Planting the
Oudolf Gardens

at Hauser & Wirth Somerset

Planting the
Oudolf Gardens

———

at Hauser & Wirth Somerset

Rory Dusoir

FOREWORD BY
Piet Oudolf

PHOTOGRAPHS BY
Jason Ingram

HAUSER & WIRTH PUBLISHERS   *filbert press*

To Hazel, who taught me about wildflowers

First published in 2019 by Filbert Press in association with Hauser & Wirth Publishers
filbertpress.com
hauserwirth.com

Text © Rory Dusoir
Photographs © Jason Ingram unless otherwise noted on page 208
Planting plans © Piet Oudolf

A catalogue record for this book is available from the British Library.

ISBN: 978-1-9997345-3-4

10 9 8 7 6   23 24 25 26 27

Designed by Michael Whitehead
Printed in China

Contents

Foreword
Piet Oudolf

It has been interesting talking to Rory Dusoir about how I set about making the garden at Hauser & Wirth Somerset. It got off to a good start when Iwan and Manuela Wirth gave me absolute freedom, with no compromises, to do exactly as I wished with the 1.5 acre field behind the gallery. The fact that the garden was to be an integral part of the gallery immediately gave it a sense of place and a strong feeling of belonging to an exciting world where beautiful things happen both inside and outside.

The concept was for three distinct gardens: the farmyard which has been planted very simply with pasture retained in keeping with the buildings' history; the Cloister Garden which is an enclosed contemplative space; and the Oudolf Field which only reveals itself once you are inside the gallery. The Oudolf Field features four distinct areas: a robust perennial planting, a wet area, a group/block planting and the sporobolus meadow which evokes the feeling of walking among wild flowers.

Every gardener faces the same questions when they set about making a new garden. What do I want it to look like? What atmosphere do I want to achieve? How will I move around it? Which plants should I use? A highlight of this book is its focus on one garden which allows for close scrutiny of the design, plant selection and maintenance, illustrated by beautiful, living examples.

BELOW: The Oudolf Field is the
great set piece of the gardens at
Hauser & Wirth Somerset.

Rory's insightful commentary on the planting over the course of a year and Jason Ingram's captivating images are instructive. By inviting us to consider the overviews and plant combinations in all four seasons we begin to understand how it changes, always offering something new. Visitors frequently declare winter their favourite season of all in the garden and I can see why as I leaf through the winter section of the book.

I always see the finished garden in my mind's eye from the beginning and then work out how to fulfil this vision, building it up in sketches, layer by layer. It has been interesting for me to revisit the process in this book and review the choices and decisions that had to be made at every stage of the garden's development. At the outset, my vision for the garden was that people will hang around in it; they won't just want to come to the gallery but they will also want to be in the garden. I hope this book encourages you to hang around repeatedly in the garden at Hauser & Wirth Somerset and that it helps clarify a vision for your own garden.

Piet Oudolf
Hummelo, May 2019

OPPOSITE, TOP: *Dianthus carthusianorum* takes centre stage in the Oudolf Field in early summer, set in a matrix of prairie dropseed grass, *Sporobolus heterolepis*.

OPPOSITE, BELOW: The sporobolus grass takes on a greater prominence as the year progresses, playing a dominant role here in autumn.

Introduction
Piet Oudolf at Hauser & Wirth Somerset

'Long live the weeds and the wilderness yet.'
Inversnaid, **Gerard Manley Hopkins**

At the beginning of the 21st century it is especially poignant to hear an early voice from the Victorian Age, already fearing the encroachment of industrial society on nature. Since the Industrial Revolution, consciousness of the importance and vitality of wild spaces has become increasingly acute as they become scarcer. Where the focus of garden-making in the pre-industrial age was straightforwardly inward-looking, to create an ordered refuge from the dangers of the wider world, people now wish their gardens to form a strong connection with the natural environment in which they are set.

OPPOSITE, ABOVE: The Oudolf Field bathed in autumnal evening light. Although a tightly controlled and cultivated space, at times such as these it is hard to discern the boundary with the wider landscape.

OPPOSITE, BELOW: *Lysimachia ephemerum* silhouetted in winter against the sere flower stalks of *Sesleria autumnalis*.

The Irishman William Robinson, the horticultural arm of the Arts and Crafts movement, was perhaps the first to consciously propound a 'natural' style of gardening. He waged an ideological war against what now seem quite harmless adornments of the Victorian Age, such as standard roses or topiary, and gardened in a style that was certainly more ecologically aware than was prevalent at the time. Viewing the vast swathes of carpet-bedding that populated contemporary gardens as wasteful and artificial, Robinson popularized the concept of meadow gardening and bequeathed a strain of naturalism to English horticulture that has persisted to this day, spreading far beyond our shores.

OPPOSITE: The monochrome seedheads of *Eupatorium maculatum* 'Atropurpureum' in autumn, with *Aruncus* 'Horatio' ablaze in the background. Decaying plant material can contribute colour contrasts to a surprising degree.

FOLLOWING PAGES: Long after its joyful spring flowering, the spectral form of *Monarda bradburiana* maintains a characterful presence amid the dry brush strokes of the grass *Sporobolus heterolepis*.

LEFT: *Gillenia trifoliata* flowerstems in autumn. Piet's work instills in the viewer an appreciation of plant form that transcends the seasons.

Society has changed immeasurably since Robinson's day, and the preservation of the increasingly beleaguered natural world has become ever more urgent. Therefore, it is not surprising that the 'natural' approach to gardening should have been re-invigorated. Willingly or not, Piet Oudolf finds himself in the global vanguard of an ecologically inspired movement in horticulture. In perfecting a style that could trace its origins to post-war continental Europe, he has become perhaps the most influential figure in horticulture of his generation. His project at Hauser & Wirth Somerset deserves to stand alongside his other landmark public gardens such as the High Line and the Lurie Garden in New York and Chicago respectively; as such, its completion is a globally important event, and not only for his fellow gardeners.

Piet Oudolf and naturalistic planting

The concept of naturalistic planting is inherently paradoxical, for gardening, by definition, asserts control over the environment to a greater or lesser degree. Piet would be the first to admit that if left to nature, his gardens would not survive for much more than one season; they originate from a strong vision, and hard work is required to maintain them after the installation is complete. You could make the argument that his design intent is as clear-sighted as that of Le Nôtre and that rigid control post-installation is equally essential for its continuation. Although plants may occasionally be allowed their head under certain circumstances, Piet's gardens are in fact extraordinarily stable when maintained correctly. This is especially remarkable when you consider that his plant palette is dominated by herbaceous plants that as a group are notoriously mobile, fickle and ephemeral.

An 'imitation' of nature would also be a curious description of Piet's work. Nature is by definition wild and chaotic and will dominate a space with its own agenda if allowed. Gardens can perhaps best be considered as 'in-between' spaces that allow us to express our relationship with the wider world and enter into a dialogue with nature, interfere as we do with the stuff of it – trees, rocks and flowers. But whereas landscape designers such as André Le Nôtre chose to express an overt dominance over the landscape, with plenty of the straight lines that William Robinson abhorred, Piet's work presents, outwardly at least, a reverence for the haphazard beauty of the natural world. Control is a given in any horticultural endeavour, but Piet's achievement has been to fashion such an intricate, intimate system of creating and controlling artificial plant communities that he appears to work with a light touch, expressing a harmony with wilderness rather than dominance. The paradox is that the closer we lean towards nature in gardening, the more complex and thoughtful must become our means of maintaining 'order'. Piet has said, 'I try to create nature as you would wish to see it.' The implication of this is that his landscapes present a stylized evocation of nature, crystallized for human enjoyment. In some cases the stylization can be presented quite overtly, as we shall see when we look at the Hauser & Wirth gardens in more detail.

'My biggest inspiration is nature; I do not want to copy it but to recreate the emotion.'
Piet Oudolf

One of Piet's primary motivations is to provide unobtrusive settings in which the character of plants can be expressed and contemplated throughout the seasons.

ABOVE, LEFT TO RIGHT: *Chaerophyllum hirsutum* 'Roseum'; the spring growth of *Gillenia trifoliata*; *Euphorbia griffithii* 'Dixter' and *Dodecatheon jeffreyi* flower amid the undergrowth of the Cloister Garden.

BELOW: The early summer glory of the Oudolf Field featuring a strong foliage combination in the foreground of *Amsonia hubrichtii*, *Aster tataricus* 'Jindai' and the red grass *Imperata cylindrica*.

Since Robinsonian times at least, English gardening style has had a recognizable relationship with wild plant communities. Today, for all their bedding-out and pyrotechnical colour clashes, Robinson-inspired gardens such as Great Dixter and Gravetye Manor (the reinvigorated erstwhile seat of Robinson himself) nonetheless embrace nature warmly. Wild flowers run right up to the front door of Great Dixter, and a nature-inspired spirit of spontaneity coupled with a deep-seated respect for plant form influence the siting of every plant in the garden. Self-sowing plants appear to romp directly from the meadows into the borders. So how does Piet's style depart from what could have been considered the prevailing orthodoxy upon his arrival in horticulture?

One key to understanding the difference is that the creation of his style was partly driven by societal changes. What we may call 'English' gardening evolved with the chief purpose of adorning large country houses at a time when skilled labour was cheap and plentiful. Flowerbeds were called 'borders', and invariably they bordered some type of architectural feature or boundary imposed on the landscape. Piet enjoys working on public gardens in particular and has a relish for broad open

BELOW: The intensely crimson shoots of *Imperata cylindrica* amid the delicate tracery of *Sporobolus heterolepis* in flower.

LEFT: A hallmark of Oudolf's style is the acceptance of decay. *Echinacea pallida* 'Hula Dancer', set in a matrix of *Sporobolus heterolepis*, is allowed to make a telling contribution throughout the seasons, from June until the following February.

spaces; as a result his style has often been described as more democratic. An important aspect of the changes in our society is that skilled horticultural labour is now expensive and in some areas hard to come by. Unless householders are particularly wealthy, it is unlikely that they will be able to afford the constant labour and expertise required to maintain a garden in the style of Great Dixter. In response, Piet has developed a style that, while far from maintenance-free, is much more economical in terms of its ongoing labour requirements.

Piet's plantings are meticulously thought out, but once installed require much less intervention than a traditional 'English' garden. Related to this is perhaps the biggest single difference between the two styles. English gardening, at its heart, worships youth and yearns for eternal spring – for as long as possible it attempts to conceal all signs of ageing and decay. It presumes that gardeners will be on hand to remove the blemishes of age by timely cutting back or by digging up spent plants and replacing them with fresh ones. Crab apples, rose hips and the autumn colours of trees may be enjoyed; borders left to stand over winter and the skeletons of cardoons appreciated; nonetheless the prevalence of colour and freshness will be maintained for as long as possible, and autumn is ushered in grudgingly. Maturity and decay are not part of the visual language of English gardening for as long as they can possibly be avoided or concealed. But Piet's work focuses on the beauty of herbaceous plants after they have 'performed' as much as while they are still in colour. At no point in their life-cycle are they taken off-stage – the point is to relish their appearance at all stages of their growth. An Oudolf garden in winter has reached its climax, rather than undergoing an intermission.

Although the horticulture required to maintain Piet's gardens is less dynamic and demanding in the sense that his style promotes stability and as little manipulation as possible, the enhanced seasonality of his approach ushers in a new type of dynamism, where plants are allowed to do more of the work themselves. Perhaps nowhere can we be more aware of time passing than in a Piet Oudolf garden in the autumn, when each day alters the hue of maturing grasses by a semi-tone, each minute the light shifts its patterns. The effects of time are welcomed clear-sightedly and there is no sense of clinging on to passing glories, so that even amid the heightened consciousness of continual change we are allowed to feel contemplative and in the moment.

An early autumn scene in the Oudolf Field. This is perhaps the time of year when the seasonal dynamism of Oudolf's masterpiece can be most appreciated. While certain elements, such as the umbellifer *Selinum wallichianum* remain fresh, the prevailing sense of decay reflects the true nature of the season. The all-enveloping haze of *Sporobolus heterolepis* becomes warmer in colour as it dries, in step with the autumn sunlight. As the soft tissue of plants such as *Echinacea pallida* 'Hula Dancer' and *Phlomis russeliana* withers away, their form becomes a stronger and more terse expression in silhouette.

The genesis of the gardens

Oudolf's two most important projects previous to Hauser & Wirth Somerset, the High Line and the Lurie Garden, are set in a decidedly urban milieu. The former, an elevated freight railway that was abandoned in the early 1980s, snakes its way through skyscrapers and a post-industrial landscape on the west of Manhattan Island, while the latter is a large-scale rooftop planting in downtown Chicago. There is no doubt that some of the effectiveness of the plantings is derived from the contrast inherent in their setting. Something appearing so wild, alive and dynamic is bound to be a welcome sight in the midst of these concrete jungles.

The locality of the gardens at Hauser & Wirth Somerset could not be more different. Iwan and Manuela Wirth had purchased an abandoned farm, Durslade Farm, on the outskirts of Bruton in rural Somerset and decided to create an art gallery there. At an early stage of the project, Piet was engaged informally by the Wirths through the offices of a mutual acquaintance. Ideas for the garden evolved very much in parallel with the conceptual development of the new gallery buildings and there was a lot of discussion between Piet and the conceptual architect for the project, Luis Laplace. Piet was allowed a great deal of freedom in his design, although it was decided early on that the main set piece of the garden, which was to become the huge perennial meadow known as the Oudolf Field, should remain a surprise, unseen by gallery visitors until they stepped into it. The whole project seemed to evolve serendipitously, powered by good will, trust and a spirit of collaboration. Crucially, Piet was allowed to have involvement from an early stage.

OPPOSITE, TOP: The site for the Oudolf Field prior to planting. As one field among many in the Somerset countryside, it offered comparatively little in terms of context for the design.

OPPOSITE, BOTTOM: The completed planting plan for the Oudolf Field. Piet relished the freedom of the site and of the brief.

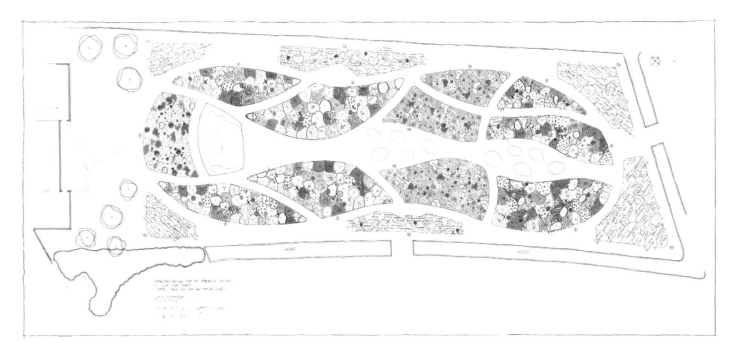

The Wirths showed Piet the 6000-sq-m (7175-sq-yd) field at the rear of the gallery and enquired how much space he would need; he asked for all of it without a second thought. The next bold decision was to fill the area almost exclusively with herbaceous perennials. Very few designers, confronted with such an open and comparatively featureless space, would rely on herbaceous plants to give it shape and meaning, yet very little in Piet's design is allowed to impose itself on the eye beyond this: there is a gaunt scattering of Kentucky coffee trees (*Gymnocladus dioicus*) on the apron of grass adjacent to the gallery, a low-key, central hoggin path, a pond and a discreet mixed native hedge forming the boundary of the site as though this were just another farmer's field. Unmissable, though, is the Radić Pavilion, a giant pebble-like structure that was brought from its first location at the Serpentine Gallery in Hyde Park but may as well have been deposited by aliens. It now acts as a slightly off-kilter focal point at the end of the garden. This extraordinary structure arrived after the garden's completion, with Piet's blessing – another serendipitous occurrence.

OPPOSITE: The Radić pavilion was a serendipitous later addition to the landscape. Its irregular, curvaceous form suits the Oudolf Field well.

BELOW: A view of the Oudolf Field facing back towards the gallery, featuring Piet's grass mounds.

Planting plans

To specify plants for such a vast series of flowerbeds in one area, Piet regards it as important to have a succession of ideas. Although the Oudolf Field is to be taken in as one piece, there are distinctive modulations throughout and a compelling sense of progression. Broadly speaking, there are three or four distinct zones, each representing a different type of vegetation within the planting. Once the overarching conceptual framework for the site has crystallized in his mind, Piet starts to work on plant lists for each area. He begins by rifling through catalogues and books to bring plants, many of them old friends, to the front of his mind. Initially he will make a long list of plants that suit the conditions and character that he envisages, then, by culling as ruthlessly as required, he arrives at a number that he is happy to work with. This rigorous honing process is perhaps ultimately as important as the detail of positioning the plants within the beds. The plant selection determines the character of each area; by drawing plants together in certain combinations and in wider communities, Piet is able to articulate ideas which are as strong as they are ineffable.

Piet's planting plans, although chiefly a means to an end, are often admired for their graphic qualities. Indeed, when Hauser & Wirth Somerset held its grand opening, the Wirths insisted that gallery space be given to a collection of his plans for the garden. Although the end goal is the creation of something to be experienced in all four dimensions, this draughtsmanship stage is important. Piet does most of his design at his desk, relying on strong powers of visualization cultivated over years of working with plants. As his way of planting is at times quite intricate and multi-layered, it is important that there is a clear visual language to describe this on paper. He prefers to draw at a scale of 1:100, as he has an instinctive grasp of how this transfers to the ground. His first step is to create distinctive symbols for each of the

BELOW: The bare bones of the layout for the Oudolf Field. The overall plan provides the conceptual framework for a collection of contrasting 'plant communities'.

OPPOSITE: Plant 'hieroglyphics' (above) and the completed planting plan for beds 1–4 in the Oudolf Field (below). Piet begins by creating suitably contrasting symbols to represent each plant on his list. These allow him to create clear and expressive planting plans which are objects of beauty in their own right.

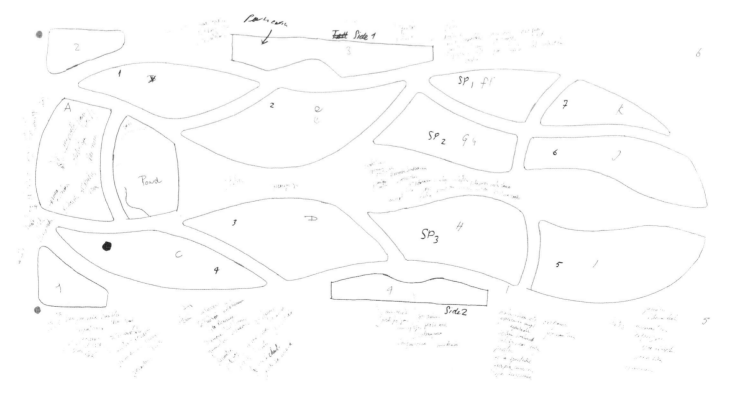

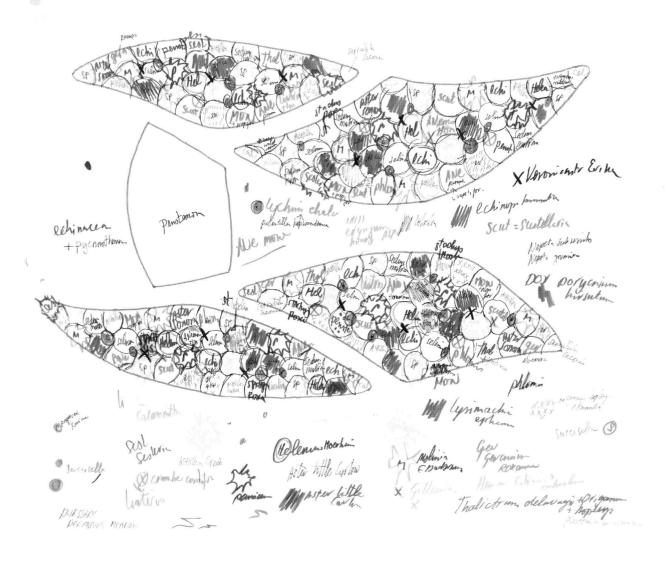

plants. Although these may reflect some aspect of the plant that they represent (colours may be roughly matched, for instance), any thought of verisimilitude is of course subservient to clarity of draughtsmanship. Elements of an interspersed, matrix-type planting are represented by open, dotty symbols, whereas blocks tend to be presented more solidly, with clear lines showing the boundaries of these distinctive plant groups. Thus, the same plants used in various ways can be represented quite differently. For example, the grass *Sporobolus heterolepis* and *Echinacea pallida* 'Hula Dancer' are meant to be interspersed in the Sporobolus Meadow and in the drawing are open and dotty; in other beds where they are planted in discrete blocks they are drawn with a firm line around them.

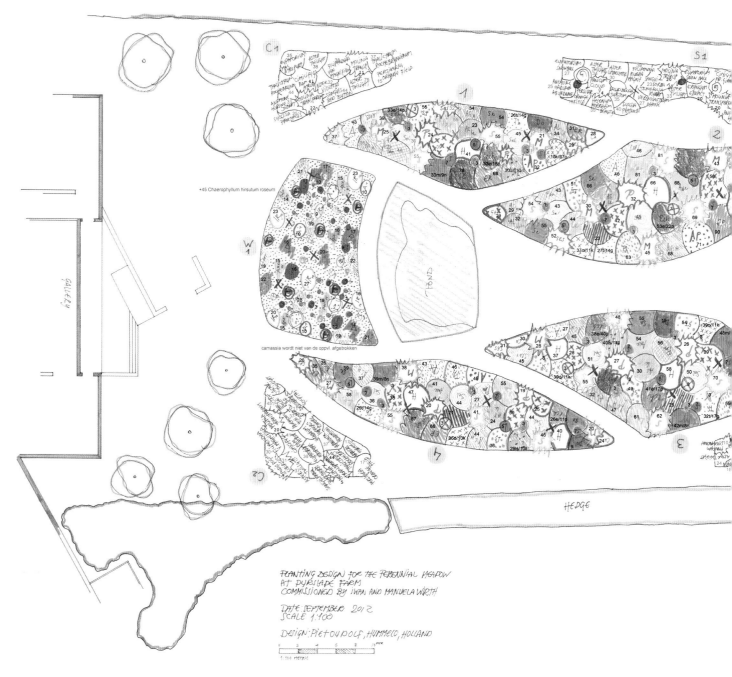

In order to facilitate implementation of the design, Piet transfers the drawings to a computer design programme such as CAD or SketchUp which allows him to quickly work out the areas covered by the plants. It only remains for him to input the planting densities and spreadsheets are then generated detailing the number of plants required in each area per variety. Piet prefers to plant thickly, as this not only allows the garden to look showy as soon as possible after planting, but also helps to prevent the incursion of weeds. Twenty-six thousand herbaceous plants were required for the implementation of the Hauser & Wirth garden as a whole.

The completed plan for the Oudolf Field. Each group of beds is accompanied by a key and a plant list.

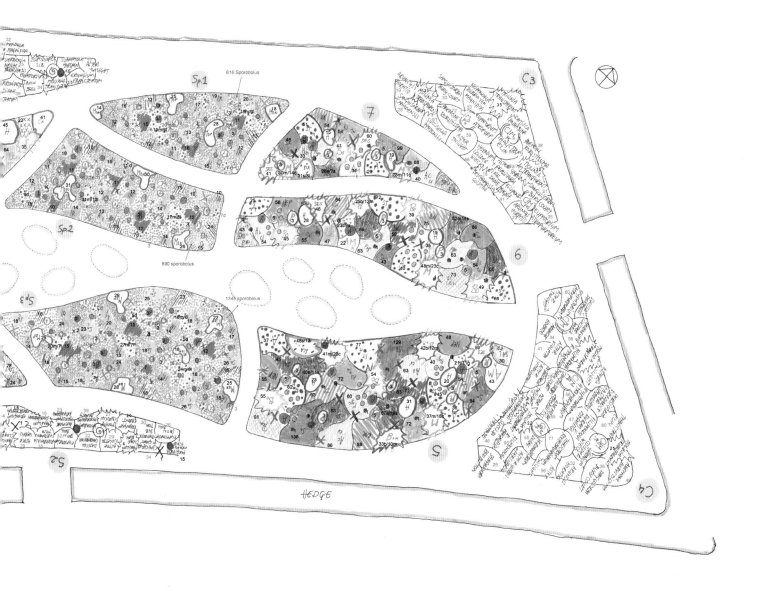

Growing the plants

Every single plant for the Hauser & Wirth garden was grown to order by Orchard Dene Nurseries in Henley-on-Thames, with a year's notice. The nursery was approached initially by the on-site landscape architects Petherick Urquhart and Hunt (now Urquhart and Hunt), who had overall responsibility for implementing Piet's design, but Piet had worked with Orchard Dene before and was more than happy with the choice. Chris and Toby Marchant, the proprietors, knew that Piet's plant choices are precise and very deliberate and to supply even a slightly different variety of the specified plant would be to compromise his design. Not surprisingly, there were challenges; a number of the plants were not in circulation in the UK wholesale market, so that the stock material had to be sourced from elsewhere. Plants such as *Monarda bradburiana*, *Aster tataricus* 'Jindai', *Amsonia hubrichtii* and *Datisca cannabina* were not broadly available at the time, but have become more popular since, quite probably due to their successful use in the gardens. And some were tricky; plants such as *Eryngium alpinum* do not overwinter well in pots, so losses or uneven growth had to be allowed for and in the case of some plants the nursery grew as many as 20 per cent extra. An added layer of difficulty was that Piet always specifies that the plants be supplied small, in 'P9s', a 9cm (4½in) square pot. This allows Piet to design more fluidly but presents timing challenges for the grower as there is a much smaller margin for error.

Orchard Dene's involvement didn't stop at the nursery gates; part of their brief was to lay out the plants on site. After a six-month delay to the planned installation date, planting took place in the spring of 2014, which was one of the wettest on record in Somerset. Herbaceous plants are rather hard to distinguish in the early spring,

The planting early in its first year. Installation had to take place in stages due to construction work on the gallery. There is plenty of bare earth visible in the first season.

Before the plants knit together the beds are particularly vulnerable to the incursion of weeds, and must be kept clean.

and although the plants were carefully labelled, there was still the possibility for confusion. Moreover, the gallery was still a construction site at the time. The Oudolf Field was planted in a three-part sequence in order to work around other contractors, which added a further layer of complication to the logistics of supplying the plants. To aid the transferral of the designs from paper to ground, the Urquhart and Hunt team created a grid of 2 x 2m (6½ x 6½ft) squares in string. This allowed the outlines of each plant group to be spray-painted onto the ground so that the planting would accurately reflect the plan.

Chris and Toby were, unsurprisingly, quite overcome when they returned to the site at its opening six months later. Having worked so hard in all that mud, they found it very rewarding to see the plants starting to reach their potential and fulfil Piet's vision.

BELOW: Plants being laid out for the Sporobolus Meadow. The gaps in between the spray-painted groups will be filled with the sporobolus grass (pictured in trays at bottom left) to form a matrix planting.

ABOVE: View back towards the gallery with planting underway.

BELOW: Planting in the Cloister Garden at its inception (left) and one year later (right). Although the main body of the flowerbeds is contained within metal edging, outlying clumps of the grass *Sesleria autumnalis* blur the boundaries and create the illusion of a naturally self-sowing plant colony.

The layout of the Oudolf Field

Piet prefers not to lay out his flowerbeds in a linear fashion, as this tends to encourage the viewer to walk past plants without stopping to look. Although the outline of the Oudolf Field is a roughly rectilinear 'field' bordered by a hedgerow, and there is a broad central walk leading to the pavilion, there are no straight lines in the layout and meandering is encouraged, if not enforced, by various obstacles. Transverse paths, rather than setting off at right angles, divert perambulating visitors almost subconsciously round to the 'sides' and 'backs' of beds. But really, it is wrong to speak of the 'backs' or 'fronts' of any of these beds, because they are designed to be viewed from all angles.

The concept of the 'island bed' was promoted in the UK by Alan Bloom in the 1970s. Although backed up by sound horticultural theory, it perhaps never quite gained enough traction to challenge the orthodoxy of English garden design. The very term 'flower border' implies a linear planting along the edge of something. The upshot of this is a more or less tiered arrangement of plants with the tallest at the back and usually a boundary-defining hedge or wall behind. Exposure to the sun and wind is therefore restricted, often resulting in the necessity to stake. It is counter-intuitive that greater exposure to the wind should enhance a plant's ability

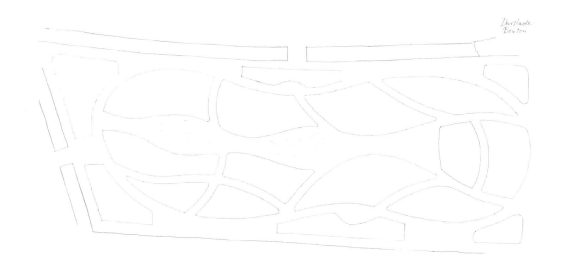

Oudolf prefers to avoid rectilinear arrangements as they encourage visitors to progress past plants rather than looking at them. With plants in full growth the grass paths are barely visible, and one feels completely immersed in the scene.

to remain upright unaided, but the truth of this is demonstrated emphatically in the Oudolf Field, where in a very open, windy situation, plants are never staked and never flop. This may be partly attributed to Piet's careful choice of plants – he has spent a lifetime curating a plant palette that is robust and low maintenance. But many of the same species and cultivars would flop forward, reaching for the light, if planted without the benefit of staking in a traditional English 'border'.

Part of Piet's mission throughout his career has been to create landscapes that are colourful and dynamic but require less maintenance than the great set-pieces of Edwardian horticulture. Avoidance of staking, that most fiddly and time-consuming of tasks, is non-negotiable – therefore it is logical that growing plants with full exposure to the elements should become a part of his design paradigm. Moreover, openness is a defining characteristic of the habitats, whether European meadow or American prairie, that generated Oudolf's plant palette in the first place. The term 'island bed' implies isolation and for this reason it is not quite right for the Oudolf Field. The beds here are in close proximity and designed to be part of a cogent whole. As well as encouraging the contemplation of plants as individuals, the obliquely angled paths allow the viewer to feel immersed in the planting. A noteworthy characteristic of the traditional English border is in general how much better it looks when viewed along its length rather than when viewed at a perpendicular angle. This is because the long view is filtered through a much greater depth of planting, gaps are less apparent, and the border appears much fuller. However, you can get the benefit of this sort of view from almost anywhere within the planting at the Oudolf Field. Wherever you walk you are able to see the whole site, filtered through a constantly modulating haze of vegetation in the foreground and middle distance. Viewpoint succeeds viewpoint kaleidoscopically as you progress through the garden without any prescribed route. On each circuit, you are enticed to follow a slightly different course.

A number of Piet's earlier projects were populated by clipped evergreens, which functioned as an unchanging sculptural counterpoint to the swirl of seasonal dynamism that surrounded them. There is nothing of that sort here, but the mounds of mown grass that occupy the open space at the centre of the meadow could be considered an understated equivalent. Piet felt it was important that this wide space, originally considered as a location for events, should be occupied to maintain a sense of balance.

Although Piet sometimes sanctions the use of metal supports, all forms of staking are absent from the gardens here at Hauser & Wirth Somerset. There would be very little opportunity to hide the apparatus of staking as all the plants can be viewed from almost any angle – moreover as the year turns, growth becomes ever more transparent.

Landscape design

Piet Oudolf is known as a plantsman first and foremost. An important part of his life's work has been to grow and continually reassess herbaceous plants, whether as a commercial nurseryman or as a garden proprietor, with ongoing experimentation at Hummelo, his own garden. It is impossible to imagine his career without this, but Piet is quick to point out that he designs landscapes and is not just a creator of planting schemes. Granted, the layout of the Oudolf Field could probably only come from the mind of a plantaholic who is intent on making plants the star of the show; nevertheless, the disposition of the beds is an indivisible part of the overall picture, and supports the effectiveness of details within the planting.

On a larger scale, Piet and the architect team have taken into consideration the visitor's journey through the whole site. The Oudolf Field, by far the most important, largest and most complex single element of the landscape, was conceived as a 'surprise' which should only be encountered towards the end of one's progression through the gallery; to lay the groundwork for this, the entrance is rather low key. The first thing you see from the car park are the raised beds which function as a kitchen garden for the restaurant. The gallery is accessed via a partially enclosed yard, where care has been taken to preserve the original character of this area as a farmyard. The biggest 'garden' gesture here was to create a flowerbed where there was once a grassy bank by discreetly retaining it with a stone wall. The planting here is quiet but effective, featuring two multi-stemmed magnolias and an herbaceous matrix which includes the tall grass *Spodiopogon sibiricus*.

BELOW, LEFT: The farmyard prior to development. The old farm buildings now contain offices, an education space, a guesthouse, galleries and a restaurant.

BELOW, RIGHT: The farmyard today with the new flowerbed, featuring the colonizing grass *Spodiopogon sibiricus* and multi-stemmed magnolia.

The Cloister Garden

At the heart of the gallery complex is the Cloister Garden, which is the next 'gardened' area that visitors encounter. Although it is a quiet, contemplative space, it is planted much more elaborately than the farmyard. In many ways it forms the perfect counterpart to the Oudolf Field: the space is enclosed and primarily defined by the architecture which surrounds it; woody plants play a key role in the structure of the planting; and the growing conditions are sheltered and somewhat shady. This space presents a number of design constraints where the Field presents very few, but Piet has managed to turn these to his advantage to create a very special garden with a strong character of its own.

The most important element of the planting in the Cloister Garden is the four multi-stemmed paper mulberry (*Broussonetia papyrifera*) trees. These respond directly to the rather awkward shape of the space in between the buildings and immediately soften its angularity. The beds beneath the trees temper this angularity still further – globular pools of vegetation are laid out under each of the mulberries, and the delineation of the beds is muddled by grasses being allowed to colonize the surrounding gravel. There appears to be a clear hierarchy governing the space – from the architecture to the trees, to the herbaceous flora – but each interaction can also be considered a dialogue. At the end, the disposition of the herbaceous beds is a clear reflection of the architecture that surrounds them, but without a straight line or awkward angle in sight; the space feels very comfortable and atmospheric.

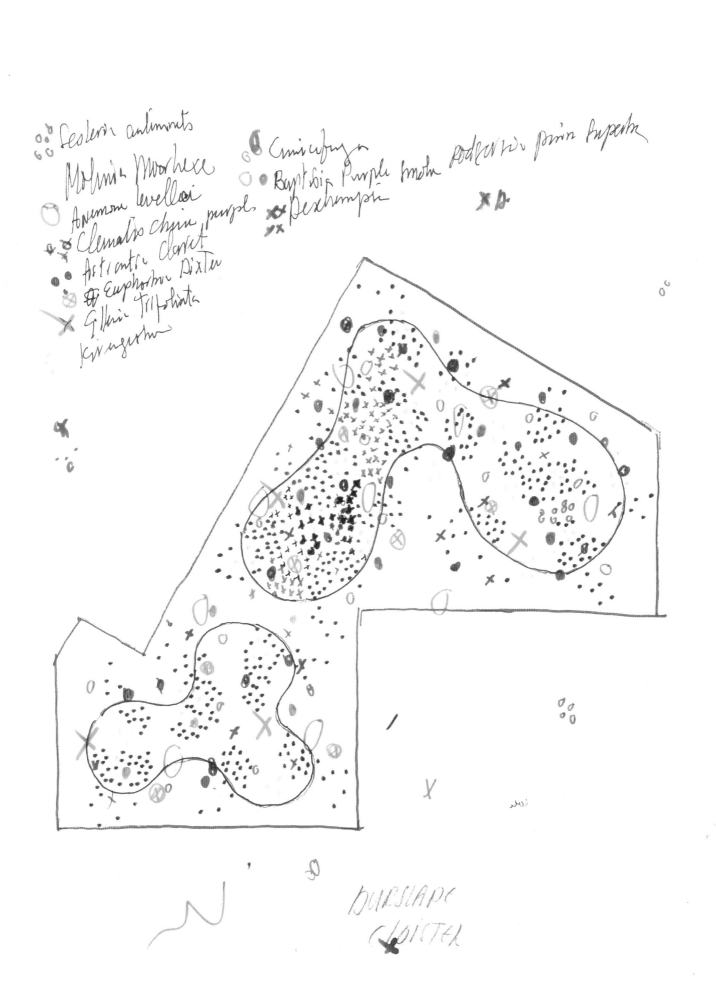

The Cloister Garden has a rarefied atmosphere, and a key to this is the carefully curated plant palette. It is essentially a matrix-planting amid the moor grass *Sesleria autumnalis*. Used en masse in a confined area, the grass has a subtly enchanting quality – the green leaves have chartreuse overtones which lend an enhanced freshness and vibrancy at almost all times of year, as though the grass were photographed in technicolour. This lends a surreal quality to the planting and the space in general. The other two grasses, *Molinia caerulea* subsp. *caerulea* 'Moorhexe' and *Deschampsia cespitosa* 'Goldtau', are used more sparingly but offer subtle tonal contrasts with the *Sesleria*. The foliage contribution of the grasses and a number of other perennials (chiefly *Euphorbia griffithii*, *Cimicifuga simplex* 'Brunette' and *Kirengeshoma palmata*) are so strong and the space so well-defined and characterful that all that is required to enliven the space seasonally are comparatively small (and sometimes short-lived) dashes of dynamism and colour. These come from the flowering of the euphorbia and kirengeshoma themselves, and the beautiful growth and flowering of *Gillenia trifoliata*. Fittingly, for what is essentially a stylized woodland garden, bulbs are also important in this regard.

The bulb selection is rather special: *Scilla peruviana*, with its extraordinary large, pyramidal flowerheads; *Dodecatheon jeffreyi*, a tall, clear pink form of the American primrose relative known as the shooting-star; *Nectaroscordum tripedale*, an achingly choice bulb – another of these *Allium* relatives, *N. siculum*, features in the perennial meadow, but *N. tripedale* is a rare and exquisite beast which takes its place quite nonchalantly in this refined setting. *Lilium martagon* contributes as much with its well-structured foliage as with its reflexed flowers.

ABOVE, TOP LEFT: The grass *Sesleria autumnalis*, with its chartreuse coloration, casts a subtle spell over the Cloister Garden.

ABOVE, BOTTOM LEFT: A somewhat awkwardly angular space is rendered relaxing and comfortable by skilful planting.

ABOVE, RIGHT: *Deschampsia cespitosa* 'Goldtau' with its veil-like inflorescence in June.

Piet creates a long list of possible plants to use in a certain area, honing it down as the design progresses. In such a small area as this, restraint in plant selection is particularly important, as every plant must make a contribution if it is not to muddle the intended effect. Piet's treatment of this space has a sculptural quality in that the objects within it (plants, in this case) unify the space and give it meaning; the disciplined choice of plants makes a vital contribution to the overall impression.

The appreciation of space and the presentation of a heavily stylized 'landscape in miniature' are reminiscent of the Japanese approach to gardening, although expressed in a different medium and with different rules. Piet's planting has an ecological quality and seasonal dynamism that is not present in Japanese gardens. Vegetation is the primary, indeed almost the sole, subject of the mini-landscape here, which is not the case with traditional Japanese gardens. Piet's reputation as a plantsman can occasionally overshadow all else, to the extent that he is sometimes referred to as a 'planting designer'. However, this does not do justice to the strength of his ability to understand and manipulate space, which is amply demonstrated here. Although his preferred medium happens to be plants rather than hard landscaping elements, his acute spatial awareness is crucial to his work. Garden-orientated visitors to the Hauser & Wirth gallery will tend to make a beeline for the Oudolf Field and will be impressed by the scale of the planting, for which more than 26,000 perennials were installed. Many will conclude that vast amounts of open space are required to emulate the Oudolf style. But the Cloister Garden demonstrates Oudolf's adaptability and creates a pleasing balance of different approaches within the site as a whole.

ABOVE, LEFT: The contrasting forms and colours of two grasses, *Sesleria autumnalis* and *Molinia caerulea* subsp. *caerulea* 'Moorhexe'.

ABOVE, RIGHT: The contemplative nature of the space encourages appreciation of subtleties, such as the fine winter tracery of *Gillenia trifoliata*.

Stylized nature: planting in the Oudolf Field

Piet has christened his planting at the Oudolf Field a 'perennial meadow'. This sounds like a straightforward idea, but of course it is not as simple as it sounds. There is a branch of horticulture dedicated to sustaining meadow-like plant communities with minimal intervention beyond two or three cuts with a scythe every year. Piet's 'meadow' is nothing of this sort – in general the location of each group of plants was carefully considered and the garden requires daily, skilled maintenance.

If the Oudolf Field is in any sense a 'meadow', it must be pointed out that it is a meadow of many parts. At the heart of the garden is the 'Sporobolus Matrix', comprising beds beds Sp1–Sp3 on the plan (pp30-31) – a planting that mimics xerophytic grassland, adapted to an environment with little water. As such it is characterized in general by a beguiling transparency and sparsity of growth, a rather difficult trick to pull off in a fertile field in rainy Somerset. The grass *Sporobolus heterolepis*, the 'prairie dropseed', is the principle component in this planting and sets the tone with its open sward and delicate hazy flowerheads. Other notable plants are the slender but punchy *Dianthus carthusianorum* and the ethereal *Echinacea pallida*. The sub-shrub *Amorpha canescens* retains its thrifty approach to foliage production even in the generously damp English conditions and helps to create the illusion that water and nutrients are sparse.

The three main types of stylized plant communities represented in the Oudolf Field.

CENTRE: The Sporobolus Meadow in early summer (foreground). The sporobolus grass is visible as the haze in the foreground in between *Scabiosa columbaria* and *Echinacea pallida* 'Hula Dancer'. Its visibility increases later in the year.

LEFT: The beds which form a buttress around the exterior of the field have the character of ditchside vegetation and come into full growth late in the season.

RIGHT: Beds 1–7 have an intermediate character, mimicking 'mesophytic' grassland.

Beds 1–7 are full-blooded block plantings which are colourful and rather thicker in texture than the sporobolus beds, but not overwhelmingly tall or luscious in growth. To continue the ecological analogy, the plants here could be said to create the impression of a mesophytic plant community. Plants such as *Helenium* 'Moerheim Beauty', *Geranium* 'Patricia', *Salvia* × *sylvestris* 'Dear Anja' and grasses which are denser in texture such as *Sesleria autumnalis* or *Pennisetum alopecuroides* f. *viridescens* are the mainstays of these beds, which take up the greatest area of the garden.

At the corners and edges of the site are beds C1-C4 and S1–S2. Although they are spread widely over the whole site, they are analogous to one another in terms of their planting and also have it in common that they are situated toward the boundaries of the garden. The planting here resembles the flora of ditch-sides and by late summer has formed a tall barrier of luscious foliage that is impenetrable to the eye. Plants such as *Eupatorium maculatum* Atropurpureum Group, *Filipendula rubra* 'Venusta Magnifica', *Datisca cannabina*, *Aster novae-angliae* 'Violetta' and *Aruncus* 'Horatio' jostle with one another in the manner that plants do when the critical competition is for light, rather than for moisture and nutrients. The two remaining components of the meadow are the pond and its associated Wet Area, as the bed adjacent to the pond is known.

In purely visual terms, the use of different types of planting is very effective – it serves at once to unify the site as a whole, as well as providing dynamic variation within it. The transparent centre at the heart of the piece, the Sporobolus Meadow, gives way to gradually thicker textures until at the corners and sides the solidity of the planting acts as a buttress, marking the effective boundary of the garden. As well as this outward progression from transparency to solidity, there is also a parallel progression in terms of flowering season. The Sporobolus Meadow reaches peak flowering in June, quickly giving way to a rich senescent phase as the surrounding areas successively come into colour. The 'mesophytic' beds (1–7) flower strongly in July and early August, giving way to the plantings at the perimeter of the site, which save a lot of their colour until September/October. The value that Piet places on the effects of senescence becomes apparent here; far from something to be hidden or avoided, the gradually maturing desiccation of the Sporobolus Meadow casts its spell over the whole garden and is as important a part of the show as its colourful early summer phase. Transitions between these areas are carefully managed and balanced, and distinctions are not absolute – for instance adjacent areas will tend to have a small number of plants in common. In the Sporobolus Meadow where almost everything is brown and desiccated by midsummer, the late *Aster tataricus* 'Jindai' and the grass *Imperata cylindrica* remain fresh and this small aspect is important in terms of keeping the site unified.

It was a bold decision by Piet to use almost exclusively herbaceous plants over such a wide area, without the articulation and structure that woody plants can provide. However, the skilful and subtle progressions and modulations within the planting stave off the dangers of homogeneity and shapelessness, while working together to present the impression of a carefully crafted whole. There is poetry in this approach: although woody plants have elements of seasonality, perennial plants are constantly

OPPOSITE, TOP: View towards the 'buttress' bed C3 across the 'mesophytic' vegetation of bed 7. Even at this early stage of the year (early May), the vigorous growth of the ditchside vegetation is apparent.

OPPOSITE, BOTTOM: The Sporobolus Meadow adjoins the 'ditchside' vegetation in early autumn. 'Mesophytic' vegetation, populated by *Helenium* and *Phlomis*, is visible in the background in front of the gallery.

evolving and appear to live a whole lifetime in the course of each year. At the year's end, life leaves them, but their ghosts remain all winter, a feat that woody plants cannot rival.

Another intriguing aspect of the planting is the overt artifice of the 'ecological' conceit that governs it. For instance, a bed representing wetlands is placed in juxtaposition to the pond, but the link between them is no more than schematic – the pond is clearly a sealed unit and in reality, the soil here is no damper than anywhere else. Here and elsewhere in the Oudolf Field is a skilfully constructed but completely transparent illusion of different habitat types rather than a planting which reflects any intrinsic difference in conditions across the site.

Adjacent areas may have plants in common – for instance a number of key plants of the Sporobolus Meadow plant community, such as the sporobolus grass itself, *Echinacea pallida* and *Aster tataricus,* recur in the adjacent mesophytic meadows. Equally the mesophytic areas share in turn some taxa, for example *Helenium* 'Moerheim Beauty', *Aster macrophyllus* 'Twilight' and *Panicum virgatum* 'Shenandoah', with what we may call the 'ditchside' plantings (beds C1–C4, S1 and S2). This is effective visually in that it helps to bridge the transitions from one area to the next and unify the whole site. Although the ditchside beds at the margins are a world apart from the arid-looking Sporobolus Meadow, and share no plants in common, the transition via the intervening mesophytic beds is smooth and a sense of unity is preserved.

While each area has its own very distinctive character, it is intriguing to see how those plants that cross the divide into another area can be effective in a slightly different setting. As well as working from a purely visual perspective, the way that Piet has managed the transitions from one type of planting to the next answers well to how equivalent transitions might occur in wild plant communities, under the influence of a real change in conditions. In a wild or semi-wild habitat it is normal that such change does not lead to an abrupt change in the composition of the plant community – rather, species phase in and phase out gradually.

There is a sense of horticultural bravura in the way that Piet has managed to craft this carefully modulated illusion of varying plant habitats. The late Beth Chatto espoused the idea that gardens should be planted in a way that reflects the underlying conditions, and her own garden, where this approach was put into practice, has been very influential from the late 20th century onwards. Her famous gravel garden, planted on a free-draining high point in the garden on the site of the old car park, contrasts markedly with the low-lying water garden with its associated marginal aquatics and lush bankside plantings. Conversely, the Oudolf Field represents a similar variety of different plant communities on one site under entirely homogenous conditions. This reflects the reality that plants can be extremely adaptable once removed from the harsh levels of competition inherent in a genuinely wild plant community. What is our job as gardeners if not to exploit this flexibility?

View from the Wet Area towards the pond margin. The planting in this bed creates the illusion of moister soil conditions such as one might find next to a body of water in nature. However in reality the pond is sealed and has no bearing on moisture levels around it. *Darmera peltata* flowering in the foreground, with *Caltha palustris* in bloom at the edge of the pond itself.

Matrix planting in the Sporobolus Meadow

A unique aspect of the Sporobolus Meadow (beds Sp1-Sp3) within the context of the Oudolf Field is that they are planted as a matrix rather than in the block planting style of the rest of the garden. In this sense, of all the beds the Sporobolus Meadow bears the closest resemblance to an actual meadow, where the ebb and flow of competition between plants is allowed greater play. The supple, fluid nature of its composition aligns with its diaphanous texture to create an impressionistic counterpoint to the more substantial qualities of the beds surrounding it. This transparency right at the heart of the garden is key to the design, as it permits unbroken views across the whole site, while imparting its own magic, like a camera's filter, upon them.

Piet has been experimenting with matrix planting for a decade or more. Broadly put, this involves the imposition of at least one layer of planting (a single species or group of species) that is consistent over a large area, from which other plants emerge incidentally. The style has been inspired by wild plant communities, especially meadows, in which a species of grass, or a group of different grass species, will form a sward which is the primary, defining element of the plant community. Although dominant ecologically, it is quite often the case that the grasses (or other matrix plants) are visually subservient to other plants. In the case of a meadow, there are a couple of reasons for this: in comparison to other plants the grasses often have a fairly weak or transparent form, which is comparatively colourless; also the effect of mass repetition renders the more incidental plants automatically more interesting and striking. Therefore, paradoxically, the plants forming the matrix will have the most influence on the character and atmosphere of a planting but will be the least appreciated as individuals.

Sporobolus heterolepis, the prairie dropseed, is a native of hot, dry meadows over a broad geographical range in North America. Its use in temperate Northern Europe has been pioneered by Piet, in the face of some scepticism – in our softer climate we cannot replicate the heat and aridity of the prairies. Problems can often arise when importing species from hotter, drier climates to our own – plants may simply refuse to develop in the cooler growing season, or they may react to the greater abundance of moisture and nitrogen by growing rankly, distorting the character of the plant and making it vulnerable to damage by frost or fungal diseases. The behaviour of lavender, a Mediterranean native, in the UK is a familiar example – far from being the long-lived, sparse-growing sub-shrub that we find in the punishing conditions of the garrigue, *Lavandula* is spoiled under our conditions and will tend to grow incontinently. This leads it ultimately to splay and collapse, often succumbing to the fungal disease lavender shab.

The Sporobolus Meadow is the pre-eminent example of matrix planting at Hauser & Wirth Somerset. The grass planted en masse is extraordinarily atmospheric. Scented in the summer, it plays an increasing role as the year progresses with its ability to gather light and to act as a foil to denser objects such as the seedhead 'cones' of *Echinacea pallida* 'Hula Dancer'.

Piet experimented successfully with growing *Sporobolus heterolepis* at Hummelo and reasoned that if it was capable of growing in the Netherlands it should thrive equally in the similar conditions of the UK. It required confidence to specify it as the principle component of a significant matrix planting, as its failure in these circumstances would have catastrophically undermined the success of the garden and required a major rethink. However, the sporobolus has performed impeccably in Somerset and now defines the character at the heart of the Oudolf Field. In many ways it has proved to be the ultimate matrix plant. Its sward is crucially very open in the spring, which allows other prairie perennials the space to emerge, and possibilities for the short-lived *Dianthus carthusianorum* to self-sow. It would be unfair to describe the sporobolus as formless, for it is an elegant, shapely plant when considered as an individual specimen, and the seed-heads are structurally interesting. But due to its overall transparency, as a matrix plant its individual structure becomes elusive and is subsumed into a general haze from which other plants with more definite colouring or texture emerge prominently.

BELOW: *Dianthus carthusianorum* is a key ingredient of the Sporobolus Meadow, both in flower and in seed. However in these open conditions its propensity to self-sow means that it has to be kept in check.

Many of its companions in the meadow are similarly ethereal – *Scabiosa columbaria*, when in flower *Echinacea pallida* 'Hula Dancer' and *Dianthus carthusianorum*, *Persicaria amplexicaulis*, which in its white form 'Alba' has a slender, spidery quality, and the willowy *Amsonia hubrichtii*. But the contrasts with the few thicker-textured plants that are included are telling. *Aster tataricus* 'Jindai' has broad, coarse leaves that only seem to get greener as winter approaches and the surrounding matrix turns increasingly sere. I was curious to notice a similar effect on the natural grass verges surrounding the car park at Hauser & Wirth. Here, the deep-rooted burdock *Arctium lappa* was playing the role of the aster, somehow drawing reserves of moisture from the soil and remaining resolutely verdant when the grasses around it had shut down and become desiccated. The grass *Imperata cylindrica*, with its broader leaves and rich colouring, makes a very definite presence amid the general haziness that surrounds it. As winter approaches, the meadow resembles a photographer's radiant lightbox against which stronger plant forms are silhouetted. The sporobolus grass is an extraordinary vehicle for light and later in the year it creates a shimmering golden translucency which is flecked with the dense forms of seedheads. *Echinacea pallida* and *Dianthus carthusianorum*, which had seemed so airy and slender in flower, now embody density and strength of form. This surprising transformation typifies the dynamism that is for Piet a treasured aspect of herbaceous plants. Who could say whether he values them more for their beauty in flower or for their persistence and character in winter?

Sporobolus heterolepis appears to modulate its appearance on an almost daily basis, lending an increasing warmth as its seedheads dessicate slowly throughout the summer.

OPPOSITE: As the Sporobolus seedheads lose moisture late in the summer, they become lighter and begin to stand upright.

ABOVE: Notice the pool of light where the grass's seedheads capture the last rays of the evening sun. In the foreground note the unashamedly healthy green growth of *Aster tataricus* 'Jindai'.

Piet has remarked that a matrix is easier to design but harder to maintain than a block planting. The positioning of individual plants is much less important in the former, which approximates more closely to a wild plant community in its behaviour – here plants are expected to shift positions and self-sow over the course of time, and the effect of the whole is more important than the placement of individual plants. To be maintained successfully, this sort of planting requires knowledgeable and sympathetic maintenance by someone who understands the intention of the designer, for while plants may individually change positions or seek to dominate in one area or another, the overall balance must be maintained. For this reason, Piet is reluctant to install any matrix plantings in projects where he cannot rely on a skilled head gardener to maintain them. In a block planting, the position of each group of plants is predetermined and the intention is that they remain constant. Therefore, the vision of the designer can be upheld in a straightforward way by reference to a planting plan, without the maintenance team having to make any aesthetic decisions.

The distinction between matrix and block planting is not always a hard and fast one, but the Oudolf Field is a great place to observe the basic difference; here the bulk of the planting is done in blocks, where each variety of plant is placed in separate groups which are meant to stay put, although they will compete for space with adjacent groups. However, beds Sp1–Sp3, at the centre of the garden, are planted very much as a matrix, with the grass *Sporobolus heterolepis* being the predominant element thereof. The contrast in styles is very striking here and contributes to the dynamism and sense of progression as you explore the site. Although Piet's style has evolved latterly to incorporate matrix planting as a technique, it would be wrong to suggest that this is at the expense of block planting. In a number of projects Piet has successfully combined the two techniques to offer variation.

There are some other variations on matrix planting in the garden. The Cloister Garden and the Wet Area are both planted within a matrix of two types of *Sesleria* grass, respectively *S. autumnalis* and *S.* 'Greenlee'. In contrast to the sporobolus matrix, sesleria offers much more stability; although the way it is distributed suggests a plant that has colonized naturally, the clumps are quite static once planted.

Sesleria also offers much less seasonal variation – the flower stalks come and go but the most important contribution of this plant comes from the semi-evergreen clump of foliage, which remains in a surprisingly constant state throughout the course of the year.

The planting around the magnolia trees in the flowerbed at the entrance to the gallery offers an interesting variation on the idea of a matrix. Various perennials with a strong intent to colonize are combined, among them *Aster macrophyllus* 'Twilight', *A. umbellatus* and *Spodiopogon sibiricus*. In contrast to the Sporobolus Meadow, the grass in this matrix is structurally the most imposing plant, with *Aster macrophyllus* knitting in to all the unoccupied spaces at ground level. In time it will be interesting to see whether the strapping spodiopogon grass will have the vigour to dominate this planting more and more.

Two further examples of matrix planting.

TOP: The Wet Area was originally planted in a matrix of *Briza media* 'Limouzi', but this has been replaced with the more dependable *Sesleria* 'Greenlee'.

BELOW: The grass *Spodiopogon sibiricus* runs somewhat at the root and forms an interlocking matrix with *Aster macrophyllus* 'Twilight'.

Maintaining Piet's vision

Head gardener Mark Dumbleton, ably supported by his assistant Jasper Casey, has been in day-to-day charge of the gardens almost since their inception, and it is clear that in Piet's estimation he has made a major contribution to the success of the project. Mark has responsibility for a huge planting area, and the establishment phase of any newly planted project can be very demanding as there is plenty of time and space for weeds to become established before perennials mature and knit together. There were also some unwelcome complications in the implementation of the planting, which Mark surmounted with a combination of ingenuity and hard graft. In particular, the soil conditions were very difficult – having been compacted hard by heavy machinery in wet conditions, there was a pan not far below the soil surface which severely restricted root growth. Mark and Jasper worked painstakingly to rectify this, lifting and replanting over large areas and cultivating the soil by hand, incorporating organic matter to promote the passage of water and air through the soil. The improvement in growth in the beds where Mark has had time to do this are a testament to his initiative and hard work.

Mark's engineering background has helped him overcome a number of technical hurdles – perhaps most acutely in the scorching summer of 2018, when his improvements to the garden's water supply allowed him to keep plants going under critical drought stress. Irrigation by spring water, the system that Mark inherited, was inadequate for the garden's needs in such a difficult year. Perhaps most importantly of all, Mark is sensitive to Piet's aesthetic vision and has intuitively grasped the way in which he likes his plants to be gardened.

Mark sees himself as a custodian of Piet's creation rather than someone who should be attempting to impose his own vision. Nevertheless, his role requires him to make numerous creative decisions in order to sustain and develop the garden and of course requires an exceptional level of plant knowledge. The sporobolus matrix is a case in point; plants in a matrix are liable to shift their position or proliferate at the expense of their neighbours, but order cannot be restored simply by reference to the planting plan, which in the case of a matrix is only likely to offer a schematic guide to the location of individual plants. As innocuous-looking a plant as *Dianthus carthusianorum* can play havoc in the open texture of the sporobolus sward, and its self-sowing habits have to be curtailed. But this needs to be done judiciously, as the plant is somewhat short-lived and so must be allowed to renew itself in order to maintain the correct balance.

Piet and Mark's working relationship is all-important to the success of the project. Piet visits whenever he can to run his eye over the garden, but as he is there no more than once or twice a year there is no time for micro-management – Mark's attention to detail and horticultural knowledge must sustain the garden for 99 per cent of the time. He has made some adjustments to allow for Piet's style: for example, he used to spend a good deal of time shearing back heleniums to encourage a second flush of flowers, but after observing Piet photographing their seedheads on one of his visits he left them alone and saved himself a lot of time.

Adapting his maintenance style to that of the garden means that Mark's discussions
with Piet can focus on matters of a less routine nature, such as making ongoing
tweaks to the planting. For instance, a group of the Mediterranean sub-shrub
Dorycnium hirsutum outgrew itself and became rather a tawdry mess; concluding it
wasn't suited to the climate and soil at the garden, they decided to replace it with
something with grey foliage. Eventually a cultivar of *Artemisia ludoviciana* was
chosen, in spite of concerns that it may not be very long-lived. These are tiny
adjustments in the scale of things – plants are notoriously unpredictable in their
behaviour and it is not uncommon for wholesale changes to be made to a garden
after planting plans have been implemented. Because Piet knows his plants so well,
and because his style tends towards stability, changes at this site are very few, and
minor. Probably the biggest disappointment was the original planting in the Wet
Area of the grass *Briza media* 'Limouzi' as the main element of a matrix. It tended
to collapse, succumbing to heat in the middle of the season, and was eventually
discarded in favour of the tougher *Sesleria* 'Greenlee'.

Planting the Piet Oudolf way

If you were to ask Piet to teach you how to use plants the way he does, he would no doubt demur as his choices are very personal. He places a lot of emphasis upon creativity and is determined that every project he undertakes should be completely original. It would be impossible to produce a rationale for the way he builds planting schemes, because a lot of what he does is instinctive. As bystanders, though, it is of course instructive to observe a master of his craft in action and draw what lessons we can.

An absolutely vital facet of Piet's career is the depth of his plant knowledge. Plants, and herbaceous species in particular, have a life of their own. The range of variables that they are subject to is dauntingly large, and that is even before you start combining them with one another. When you design with plants, you work in four dimensions to a greater extent than in any other visual art form, and your subjects interact with the elements in an integral and unpredictable way. Piet's career would be impossible without a deep understanding of his materials, and with plants this can only come from a lifetime of observing and working with them. This does not preclude further innovation – he is constantly on the look-out for new plants, but these will always be absorbed into his existing plant palette thoughtfully, after a period of observing them in cultivation. In his decades-long career as a nurseryman, Piet has not only grown most of the plants he uses but has also bred many of them himself.

Herbaceous plants are so varied, dynamic and colourful that it can be difficult to make sense of them. Instinctively we look for an exterior context, an anchor point, to give them articulation and meaning. Very little of this is to be found in the Oudolf Field, but while there is a danger of such a garden degenerating into something akin to chaos, a visually indigestible mass, Piet has found a way to create rhythm, balance and meaning.

The laying out of plants is often termed 'planting design' and may be relegated to the category of a decoration, subordinate to built elements in the landscape. Piet's preference is to use numerous herbaceous plants and this can sometimes lead to the misconception that he is a 'planting designer', but his most successful projects have arisen when he has had the latitude to respond to the site as a whole. His work at Hauser & Wirth Somerset shows his understanding of space as much as his mastery of plants. The Oudolf Field is an extraordinary tour de force, demonstrating that herbaceous plants, when taken seriously enough, do have the capacity to give meaning to a wide, empty space almost by themselves, but Piet's work on the choice and placing of the plants is an indivisible part of its success.

The landscape at Hauser & Wirth Somerset bears revisiting time and time again; it is such a multi-faceted thing that one's experience of it is never quite the same from visit to visit. In the chapters that follow I shall attempt to give an impression of the garden from season to season, but really it evolves on a daily basis and always repays the effort to get there.

OPPOSITE: High summer shifts into autumn in the many-splendoured Oudolf Field. After a lifetime of cultivating and designing with plants, Piet Oudolf considers his landscape work at Hauser & Wirth Somerset one of the greatest achievements of his career to date.

Winter

In the most austere season, stripped of the vibrant colours of spring and autumn and of the distracting dynamism of growth and bright sunlight, the planting comes to exhibit an inner strength that is remarkable for a garden composed almost entirely of dead plant tissue. A sparse grouping of the fascinatingly gaunt Kentucky coffee tree (*Gymnocladus dioicus*) inhabits one end of the Oudolf Field, but the rest of the planting there is almost entirely herbaceous.

The Oudolf Field in winter, under a light frost. It is remarkable the extent to which Oudolf's selection of plants retain their character even after all green tissue has been stripped away. *Stachys officinalis* 'Hummelo', *Echinacea*, and *Datisca cannabina* stand out in particular.

BELOW: Winter skeletons have a beauty all of their own. An important part of Oudolf's work as a landscape designer has been to bring them the attention they deserve. Left to right: *Lysimachia ephemerum, Filipendula rubra* 'Venusta Magnifica', *Aster macrophyllus* 'Twilight' and *Dianthus carthusianorum*.

OPPOSITE: The composition of the flowerbeds at Hauser & Wirth Somerset reads equally well in the winter as it does in the summer.

TOP: *Sesleria autumnalis* with *Sedum* 'Matrona' in the foreground, and the dark, globular seedheads of *Phlomis russeliana* behind. BOTTOM: The russet tones of *Lysimachia ephemerum* thawed and lit up by the sun.

The English gardening tradition looks for winter solace in evergreen structure, in berried trees and shrubs, and in those plants that adapt to the variable English winter by flowering in mild spells in a pale imitation of the glories of summer. Our winter is often such a wishy-washy affair, particularly in the south, that it sometimes feels as though the creep of spring starts as soon as you have finished digging up your last dahlia for storage. From mahonia to hellebore, to snowdrop, to daphne – so we gloss over the severity of the season.

A continental winter is a weightier matter and cannot be circumvented in this way. Perhaps this is one reason why Piet Oudolf and his European cohort have been so instrumental in creating a style that embraces the solemn character of a 'real' winter. Piet has remarked in the past that 'a plant is not worth growing unless it looks good dead'. This does not merely apply to the grasses that have become so closely associated with the 'New Continental' planting style. A strict discipline governs Piet's choice of plants, so that a high proportion of herbaceous plants are expected to earn their keep in the darkest season of the year. Leaves have coloured, shattered and fallen, and the predominant colour is now brown, but the plants here leave strong bones and what remains can be seen as a culmination of the season's growth, its architecture laid bare, rather than so much mess to be cleared away. The robust, upstanding nature of the perennials Piet has chosen is appreciated now more than ever.

Winter skeletons

In the Oudolf Field, Piet entirely eschews winter structure in the traditional sense of evergreen shrubs or hedges. There is no strong formal structure or hard landscaping to provide solidity, the 'backbone' that has been considered essential to garden design for centuries. The principle woody specimens here (the group of Kentucky coffee trees), if anything, accentuate the feeling of desolation due to the uncompromising starkness of their frames. The onus therefore lies almost exclusively on the herbaceous planting to carry our interest through the winter. As much as it may have become common practice to leave grasses and other structural perennials standing (more or less selectively) until early spring, it is unusual for them to take centre stage to the extent we see here.

The importance of plant shape, which is perhaps easier to overlook at busier times of year, is now starkly exposed. Colour has not been eliminated, but the palette is severely restricted. All soft tissue has been reduced to dust, and we are invited to view the garden as if it has ossified. Rather than a pale echo of summer's growth, it feels as though the garden is stripped down to its most essential components; in the dearth of colour, scent and growth, our response to form, tone and texture is refined.

ABOVE: The silhouette of *Eryngium yuccifolium* is as unmistakeable in winter as it is in the summertime.

OPPOSITE: Leaving herbaceous plants standing over the winter has an important benefit to wildlife, providing habitat and forage for birds and invertebrates. Here *Phlomis russeliana* provides a perch.

The layout allows the viewer to take in the whole of the Oudolf Field at once. Strongly structured plants carry the eye across the garden, and there are probably few with a greater presence and personality in winter than *Datisca cannabina*, with its impressive 3m (10ft) arching shoots, hung with ragged tassles. The domed structure of *Eupatorium purpureum* makes it an important landscape feature and a constant foil to upright plants, such as the rigidly structured spires of *Veronicastrum*. Lower down, *Sedum* assumes a similar role and plays off against *Pennisetum*, *Sporobolus* and *Salvia*.

Many perennials offer structural interest throughout winter.

ABOVE, LEFT: The ghostly form of the umbellifer *Selinum wallichianum*.

ABOVE, RIGHT: The spent remains of the of swamp milkweed seedheads (*Asclepias incarnata*).

In a broad view of the landscape, some of the most visually striking elements in winter are the densest. *Echinacea pallida* 'Hula Dancer', the inflorescence reduced to its eponymous cones, remains a standout performer in the winter. Throughout the garden there is a constantly recurring interplay between the solid and the diaphanous, of which the combination of the echinacea with *Sporobolus heterolepis* is a prime example. The highly structured seedheads of *Phlomis russeliana*, which last from July, now come into their own in this newly monochromatic scene.

ABOVE, LEFT: By this stage of the year the *Sporobolus* matrix has devolved from a a radiant haze to a backdrop of fine brush-strokes, in either case a great foil for the powerful expression of form that is *Echinacea pallida* 'Hula Dancer'.

ABOVE, RIGHT: *Eupatorium maculatum* 'Atropurpureum' retains its form immaculately throughout the winter.

As well as allowing broad views of the landscape, the design of the Oudolf Field, with its meandering paths, encourages the appreciation of plants as individuals, with all their intricate variations of form and texture. This is never more so than at this most contemplative time of year. The ghostly skeletons of *Selinum wallichianum*, *Eryngium alpinum* and *Asclepias incarnata* reward attention as botanically and aesthetically intriguing structures although they have a lesser impact on the wider landscape.

ABOVE, LEFT: The persistent seedheads of *Agastache foeniculum*, with a clump of *Serratula seoanei* at its base.

ABOVE, RIGHT: The spectral form of *Eryngium alpinum* in winter.

OPPOSITE, ABOVE: The low, but emphatic winter presence of domed *Sedum* 'Matrona'.

OPPOSITE, BELOW: The tall, arching shoots of *Datisca cannabina*, draped mournfully with the tassels of summer's growth, make a dramatic statement even from some distance. It is visible in the top left corner of this picture.

Colour in winter

We are accustomed to seeing herbaceous plants in winter mainly as vehicles for the sparkly effects of frost. A good hoar frost will bring out the garden photographers in droves, and no doubt it is always exciting to view the transformative effect of cold weather on a landscape. But the overlay of frost dilutes colour and can deaden the definition between plants; once it has lifted it can be surprising how much life comes into the garden as the colours warm up in the glow of the oblique winter sun. The spectrum is, of course, much reduced. 'A symphony of brown' may not

ABOVE: The subtleties of colour variation in the winter.

LEFT: *Serratula seoanei* retains its strong, compact character throughout winter.

RIGHT: *Lysimachia ephemerum.*

OPPOSITE: Garden photographers are naturally drawn to a Piet Oudolf garden under frost – but as it thaws a surprising richness of colour variation is revealed.

OPPOSITE, ABOVE: The remains of *Aster amellus* 'Sonora' are resolutely monochrome and contrast with the warmer tones of neighbouring grasses.

OPPOSITE, BELOW: The ghostly winter form of *Amsonia hubrichtii*, this time in contrast with the russet stems of *Lysimachia ephemerum*.

BELOW, LEFT TO RIGHT: Dark *Phlomis russeliana* seedheads; *Sesleria autumnalis* retains a degree of its chartreuse coloration throughout the winter; the wiry fuzz of *Calamintha nepeta* subsp. *nepeta* contrasts with *Molinia caerulea* subsp.

caerulea 'Edith Dudszus'; seedheads of *Monarda bradburiana* bathing in precious winter light.

sound that appealing, but in straitened circumstances our eyes become more attuned to subtlety. With this adjustment, the Oudolf Field can be as much of a visual feast in winter as at any other time.

A notable feature of a deciduous grass such as *Sporobolus heterolepis* is its passive ability to transmit the warmth (in terms of colour) of the low winter sun. Given the shifting light and the deadening influence of cloud cover, this is a dynamic, mercurial effect, making it all the more precious. Even warmer tones can be found in the russet seedheads of *Lysimachia ephemerum* or the foliage of *Amsonia hubrichtii* continues to enthral in the most unexpected way, its seedheads glinting a remarkable silver.

The wiry mass of stems the *Calamintha nepeta* subsp. *nepeta* leaves behind has a hazy purple effect, contrasting nicely with the pale remains of *Sesleria autumnalis*. Other plants remain resolutely monochromatic, a particularly striking example being *Aster amellus* 'Sonora'. The blackened stems and foliage allow the remarkably persistent fluffy white aggregations of fruit to stand out by virtue of the extreme contrast.

Grasses in winter

Grasses have become indelibly associated in the public conscientiousness with Piet Oudolf's planting design and that of the New Perennial Movement of which he is at the fore. A large part of their appeal stems from their strength as winter features. Whether deciduous or evergreen, they maintain their presence and character throughout the winter better than any other group of perennials.

Evergreen grasses in the Oudolf Field are few in number and not particularly imposing. They are among the very few species in the Field that remain standing after the clearance operation. *Stipa tenuissima* is evergreen in name only, the predominant colour of its leaves being white, with only a few strands of green. Although it is less dynamic in terms of seasonal change, it is a great source of flowing movement throughout the year and this characteristic becomes particularly prominent in the winter. *Festuca mairei* and *Deschampsia cespitosa* 'Goldtau' are the other evergreen species.

Among the most imposing of all the grasses used in the garden is *Spodiopogon sibiricus*. In the Field it jostles with *Datisca cannabina* at the fringes of the garden and it also features strongly as a matrix plant in the bed that welcomes visitors as they

BELOW: *Deschampsia cespitosa* 'Goldtau' at the bottom left of the picture. Although the flower stems are now sere and spidery, the clump of basal leaves is semi-evergreen.

OPPOSITE, ABOVE: A selection of grasses in winter showing good variation in colour – reddish *Panicum virgatum* 'Shenandoah' (to the left), bleached chartreuse *Sesleria autumnalis* in the fore-ground, *Molinia caerulea* subsp. *caerulea* 'Edith Dudzus' at the back.

OPPOSITE, BELOW: *Echinacea pallida* 'Hula Dancer' seedheads arise from a sea of *Stipa tenuissima*.

enter the gallery. At the opposite end of the spectrum, *Sporobolus heterolepis* offers not so much structure as texture – with its fine, open foliage it creates a shimmering haze through which to view more solid objects.

Of the three *Molinia* cultivars the tallest, *M. caerulea* subsp. *arundinacea* 'Transparent', is the least durable and is prone to collapsing in the wind, one of very few plants in the garden that falls over. *M. caerulea* subsp. *caerulea* 'Moorhexe' and 'Edith Dudszus'

ABOVE: The fountainous grass *Pennisetum alopecuroides* f. *viridescens* forms a whispy background for the seedheads of *Stachys officinalis* 'Hummelo'.

both remain unmoved by the weather and make very fine, highly structured winter features. *Pennisetum alopecuroides* f. *viridescens* turns pale in the winter but maintains perfectly its flowing, fountain-like habit. Atypically for its genus, *Panicum virgatum* 'Shenandoah' stands exceptionally well, and it doesn't rely on direct sunlight to contribute a notably warm orange colouring.

ABOVE: *Panicum virgatum* 'Cloud Nine' is the very tall, clump-forming grass at the left of this picture. Although it doesn't possess the same warmth of colouring as 'Shenandoah', its height contributes well to the 'buttress effect' of the outer beds.

Winter work

Given that the sere remnants of summer's growth form an integral part of the yearly display, there is understandably a reluctance to embark on the hefty annual clearance operation. However, there comes a point in late January when the process must get under way for fear of starting the race too late, when bulbs and the fresh shoots of perennials are beginning to reappear. Their emergence can transform an arduous but straightforward job into something much more fiddly as new growth obstructs removal of the old, for fear of damage with secateurs or with heavy footsteps. Ultimately, the stage must be cleared in time for the next year's performance to begin.

To lessen the impact of demolishing winter's scenery, the work on the Oudolf Field starts in a certain sequence: the Wet Area in front of the pond first, where there is rather less to see in winter anyway, followed by the beds on the periphery of the garden. Perennials are cut neatly down with secateurs, to the point where nothing is visible above ground. For substantial deciduous grasses, a pruning saw is used. With a few exceptions, all traces of the previous year's growth are removed, leaving bare soil everywhere. Only the few evergreen grasses and shrubby species remain standing, to be tidied up and pruned as required.

ABOVE AND OPPOSITE: Cutting down perennials begins in late winter, a huge job given the scale of the flowerbeds in the Oudolf Field. Nonetheless the cuts are executed with precision, using secateurs, as can be seen with this *Sedum*.

The soil is invariably quite saturated at this time of year and care must be taken to minimize soil compaction. The structure of clay soil is extremely susceptible to long-term damage when wet; just one squelchy footprint can inhibit good drainage and root growth for a matter of years. A hard frost is ideal for undertaking this work, as this allows one to travel around the beds with impunity. However, a sustained period of sufficiently cold weather in south-west England cannot be reliably expected, and the sheer volume of cutting down required at this garden requires the gardeners to be resourceful and get on with it no matter what the conditions.

Paradoxically, it is usually kinder to step on dormant plants, provided their root systems are robust, than it is to stand on the open ground. The crowns of deciduous grasses in particular become a handy platform to work from, as their roots are more than strong enough to support one's weight. Moving around the beds in this way, or using wooden boards, minimizes soil damage and prevents one's boots from accumulating a lot of mud.

Spring

However much the winter landscape has been admired, its demolition brings relief to the eye as we embrace the new season. Once the huge annual tidy-up is complete, the garden is as empty as it will ever be and the slowly decaying browns and silvers of the past few months finally give way to the fresh colours of spring. Piet's borders are known for their late season; he has joked that spring is his least favourite time of year.

ABOVE: Oudolf resists the temptation to allow carpets of forget-me-nots to stitch his plantings together. As a result there are some gaps and areas of bare soil as the perennials emerge, as among the shoots of *Monarda bradburiana* (right). The focus is more on the subtle variation and beauty of emergent foliage, such as with *Imperata cylindrica* (left), and *Gillenia trifoliata* (centre).

OPPOSITE: patchworks of burgeoning foliage in the spring are already beginning to differentiate themselves in colour, form and texture. Spring is a great time to 'see' and understand the garden.

Unlike all other times of the year, all plants can be inspected from overhead.

Many of the prairie perennials that form the core of his planting are slow to rise and leave large gaps of bare soil around them as late as May. There is no overlay of forget-me-nots (*Myosotis*) to fill in all the gaps – such a rampant self-sower would need careful management if it were not to compromise the early growth of the main crop of perennials.

This would be too time-consuming over such a wide area. The competition between plants in the Oudolf Field is finely balanced – especially in an area such as the Sporobolus Meadow, where the introduction of such a heavy, carpeting weed would be catastrophic, suppressing the less obtrusive self-sowing of plants such as *Dianthus carthusianorum* and *Scabiosa columbaria*.

Myosotis can exert a sort of tyranny over the early spring scene if allowed, and its absence allows some of the more diminutive bulbs, such as species tulips and the vivid *Muscari armeniacum* 'Valerie Finnis' to thrive and be seen. Moreover, the early foliage of perennials becomes more important, not only as a foil to bulbs (which tend to look bereft emerging from otherwise empty soil), but also as objects of beauty and symbols of spring in their own right. In its own way the fresh, self-dappling spring foliage of *Aster macrophyllus* is as engaging as a colony of bulbs in bloom. The gorgeous spring emergence of the tender shoots of *Gillenia trifoliata* is something to be cherished, and it is a hallmark of Piet Oudolf's style that we are encouraged to appreciate a plant in its entirety, and not just for the moments when it is overtly 'performing'. Although Piet's appreciation for plants in their senescent phase is now well-recognized, it is perhaps under-appreciated that his landscapes are also designed to foster recognition of how interesting perennials can look as they emerge in the spring.

For those interested in the mechanics of a flower border, spring is a great time for study as the eye can take in entire beds at once, without the obstruction of tall, mature growth. One can appreciate how a bed was planted and also how gamely the plants compete. Wherever it is planted, *Aster macrophyllus* 'Twilight' runs among its neighbours, and it is important that their vigour is capable of withstanding this. In places, it is allowed to interlock and form a matrix with other willing competitors, such as *Spodiopogon sibiricus*. Where it encroaches on clump-formers such as *Eupatorium maculatum*, that plant's robust nature and superior stature are enough to see off the interloping shoots of the aster later in the season.

THIS PAGE: *Aster macrophyllus* 'Twilight' is a determined under-ground colonizer and emerges over a much larger area in spring than may have been intended! However its early growth is beguilingly delicate, and vigorous subjects, such as *Eupatorium maculatum* seen pushing through in the picture on the left and *Persicaria amplexicaulis* in the picture on the right, should be able to withstand the competition without any intervention.

Bulbs

In April, the massed planting of *Camassia leichtlinii* holds sway over the whole field. Spring bulbs that have the stature to dominate a landscape on this scale are rare, and as the planting is predominantly rather flat at this time of year, the camassia provides some welcome height. Its vigour is such that it can compete with almost anything, only perhaps losing out to the blanketing growth of *Phlomis russeliana*. *Scilla peruviana* and the elegant *Dodecatheon jeffreyi* sit well in the jewel-box that is the Cloister Garden planting, where they flower in vibrant contrast to the yellowish foliage of *Sesleria autumnalis*, which is already so lush at this early stage of the year. *Nectaroscordum tripedale* towers over both of these, with *Lilium martagon* a strong presence although it is not yet in flower. Although tiny, *Muscari armeniacum* 'Valerie Finnis' punches well above its weight in the field due to its particularly piercing pale blue colour.

ABOVE, LEFT TO RIGHT: *Dodecatheon jeffreyi*; the rare *Nectaroscordum tripedale* at its flower's birth; *Camassia leichtlinii* flowers among barely emergent clumps of perennials.

OPPOSITE, ABOVE: *Camassia leichtlinii* is the single most dominant plant in the landscape in early spring.

OPPOSITE, BELOW: the smaller scale and enchanted woodland atmosphere of the Cloister Garden lends itself to bulb displays. Here *Dodecatheon jeffreyi*, the emergent growth of *Lilium martagon* and tall *Nectaroscordum tripedale* can be seen.

Colour

Excluding bulbs, very few herbaceous plants are in flower this early in the year. A notable exception is *Darmera peltata*, the water saxifrage. Planted in the Wet Area, the flowers contrast nicely both in colour and shape with the camassias in the landscape beyond. They arise in an unlikely fashion from bare rhizomes to bloom briefly before giving way to the splendid leaves. The pond is particularly colourful at this time of year, largely due to the enthusiasm of the kingcup *Caltha palustris*, but there are also skunk cabbages to admire: *Lysichiton camtschatcensis* is a marginal aroid which draws attention with its glorious white spathe, a brief but spectacular performance. *Euphorbia griffithii* 'Dixter' in the Cloister Garden is a long-lasting perennial plant that is at its most vibrant at this time of year.

OPPOSITE: The unlikely flowers of *Darmera peltata*, flowering in the Wet Area, greet visitors as they step out of the gallery, combining well with *Camassia leichtlinii*.

BELOW: *Euphorbia griffithii* 'Dixter' is at its most vividly orange at this early point in the year.

Foliage

Aside from *Aster macrophyllus* 'Twilight' and *Sesleria autumnalis*, there are a few other plants which have a particularly interesting form at this early point in the year. The leaves of *Astilboides tabularis* unfurl majestically, some of them cocked sideways to receive morning light. Vivid green *Datisca cannabina* is jagged and full of intent as it emerges from the soil. By contrast, *Phlomis russeliana* forms a lustrous, felty carpet and covers the ground competitively in the spring. The grass *Imperata cylindrica*, well known for its brash appearance in the summer, is much more subtly animated as it emerges, with its red variegation much fainter. Of the *Veronicastrum* plants, 'Adoration' is the quickest into life and the vertical vigour of its stems is enhanced by the strongly horizontal disposition of its leaves. Although many species have barely got going in spring, a number are starting to assert their character and subtle variations in colour and incipient form can create an agreeable mosaic effect which is at least interesting, even if the scene is not as attention-grabbing as at other times of the year.

BELOW: *Astilboides tabularis* unfurling its leaves dramatically in spring, backlit by the sun.

In terms of colour, spring is a comparatively quiet time of year in the Oudolf Field. This allows more focus on subtle variations in foliage and form of the emergent herbaceous plants.

ABOVE: *Veronicastrum* 'Adoration' is up early and has a distinctively tiered structure and darkish foliage.

BELOW LEFT TO RIGHT: *Thalictrum* 'Elin' is another early riser; *Phlomis russeliana* forms a felty carpet early in the year; *Imperata cylindrica* at its subtlest in early spring; and the jagged emergence of *Datisca cannabina*.

Spring work

There is little inclincation to do intrusive work on the garden during the winter, which is as important a season of display as any other. This makes the spring a crucial and very short period in which to undertake border renovation work. The list of jobs to get on with is based on observations during the course of the year. Plants are lifted and split for a variety of reasons. Parts of the garden have struggled with a legacy of heavy soil compaction by machinery. This restricts the root growth of perennials, affecting their performance above ground and reducing their drought-tolerance. Only by lifting plants and thoroughly cultivating the soil around and underneath them, incorporating well-rotted organic matter has this problem been alleviated.

Although plants must be allowed to jostle one another and create the illusion of free competition, occasionally interventions by the gardening team are necessary to regulate plants that colonize too aggressively.

ABOVE LEFT: clumps of *Molinia*, *Aruncus* and *Filipendula*, although there are gaps in between them early in the year, will fill out and compete well in due course.

ABOVE RIGHT: Here, however, *Phlomis russeliana* is too dominant in its spread and needs to be controlled by digging up the errant shoots.

OPPOSITE: *Aster macrophyllus* 'Twilight' shows its propensity to spread around *Camassia*. Happily its foliage is not quite as smother-ing a blanket as that of the *Phlomis*.

The garden has also been beset by a proliferation of swift moth caterpillars – grubs which live in the soil and feed on plant roots and stem bases. Infestations can be quite severe, substantially reducing the vigour of plants. They are best dealt with by lifting plants and removing the caterpillars by hand. Digging up plants may also be undertaken as part of the routine maintenance of the beds, occasionally dividing plants to maintain vigour or restrict their size, or perhaps to remove the infiltrating shoots of a vigorous colonizer such as *Aster macrophyllus* 'Twilight'.

Early Summer

By the beginning of June, there is hardly any bare earth in sight. Although many of the taller subjects are yet to reach their full potential, the landscape is no longer predominantly flat, as the late-developing perennials that form the core of the planting begin to differentiate themselves in form and height. Early summer is not the core season for colour, but there are still significant numbers of plants in flower. Finally, the gardens are in full swing. This marks the beginning of a nine-month period during which the gardens are particularly full and strong.

ABOVE, LEFT TO RIGHT: A vigorous foliage combination of *Aster tataricus* 'Jindai' with the crimson grass *Imperata cylindrica*; the delicate incipient flowering of *Aruncus* 'Horatio'; the fresh glory of *Filipendula rubra* 'Venusta Magnifica'. The freshness of these latter two is very transient, but their structure will abide throughout the year.

LEFT, TOP TO BOTTOM: Although planted only sporadically, *Eremurus* 'Romance' has the stature to dominate the landscape in early summer, when many of the herbaceous plants are yet to achieve their full size.

Splashes of colour from *Allium atropurpureum*, *Salvia × sylvestris* 'Dear Anja' and *Amsonia hubrichtii*.

Although growth has yet to reach its full potential in many cases, the planting is fully knitted together and the 'buttress' beds (bed C3 is seen in the corner here) are beginning to differentiate themselves with their superior stature.

Although many English gardens seem to climax naturally in June, at Hauser & Wirth this season acts only as a prelude to the peaks of high summer and autumn. However, it is characterized by a freshness that is unique here to the time of year. In a garden that does not attempt to conceal decay, even by early July there will be signs of senescence as early contributors begin to go over. Therefore, in June there is a brief moment when everything is full and burgeoning with promise, but before age has started its corrosive work. It is good to relive this moment every year.

The rewards of the Oudolf Field layout become particularly apparent at this time. The deep beds intersected by serpentine paths encourage transverse views across large portions of the site. Therefore, although a comparatively minor proportion of plants may be in flower, with a small amount of repetition in key areas they can be seen again and again, filtered through a slightly different cross-section of the vegetation. A scattering of *Eremurus* throughout beds 1–7, or the pools of ice-blue *Amsonia*, tie the whole area together, as all can be seen from any vantage point.

OPPOSITE: *Astrantia major* 'Roma' exemplifies the season, flowering in the Wet Area in association with *Geranium* 'Spinners'. Neither of these plants contribute a great deal after flowering, but their freshness is beguiling.

ABOVE, LEFT: *Salvia × sylvestris* 'Dear Anja'. After the flowers drop the calyces still contribute colour. Above, right: *Astilboides tabularis* coming into flower in the Wet Area.

Early flowers

Bulbs still make a strong contribution this late in the year, pre-eminently the apricot foxtail lily *Eremurus* 'Romance'. Although it is pale and slender, its height is sufficient for it to preside over wide areas of the Oudolf Field. It is not quite as dominant as the camassias were in their time, but it fulfils a similar function in that its spires draw the eye across broad views of the site. Alliums are also important, although not quite as visible from afar. These are not the giant lilac pom-poms such as 'Gladiator' or 'Globemaster'. *Allium atropurpureum* is quite tall, but with very dark flowers and modest, hemispherical inflorescences. The pale chalky blue *Allium caesium* and the almost translucent *Allium christophii* take their place in the atmospheric sward of the Sporobolus Meadow rather than grabbing attention from afar.

The Sporobolus Meadow reaches the peak of its flowering in early summer, as the surrounding 'mesophytic' beds are just beginning to get going. While the helenium in the background will continue to flower throughout the summer into August, the echinaceas will go over in July, losing their colour to become structural objects.

The colourful sward of the Sporobolus Meadow in detail.

ABOVE: *Dianthus carthusianorum*.

BELOW FROM LEFT TO RIGHT: *Scabiosa columbaria* in the foreground to *Dianthus carthusianorum*, *Echinacea pallida* 'Hula Dancer' and *Lythrum virgatum* 'Swirl'; *Allium caesium* in contrast with *Imperata cylindrica*;

Amsonia hubrichtii flowering in association with *Monarda bradburiana*. Although this is peak flowering time for the Sporobolus Meadow all of the above offer something later in the season, whether

continued flowering (in the case of *Lythrum* and *Scabiosa*), foliage (*Amsonia* and *Imperata*), or structural seedheads (*Echinacea* and *Dianthus*).

The Sporobolus Meadow is one of the more colourful areas at this time of year. The primary contributors to this are pale blue *Amsonia hubrichtii* and the early-flowering soft pink *Monarda bradburiana*. These give way to the equally pale *Echinacea pallida* and *Dianthus carthusianorum* (not pale, but very slender), as the season progresses. Stronger colour comes from the foliage of the grass *Imperata cylindrica*.

The Wet Area is also in its busiest and most colourful phase in this early part of the season. *Gillenia trifoliata, Iris sibirica, Campanula* 'Sarastro' and the pink umbel *Pimpinella major* are all in full flower. The adjacent pond also contributes strongly, with a fringe of the tall flowering rush *Butomus umbellatus* and at a lower level the bright yellow kingcup *Caltha palustris*. These two areas both catch the eye but have starkly contrasting characters, the one with its open, ethereal character populated by pastel colours, the other much more luscious in growth and bustling with vibrancy.

BELOW: The 'flowering rush' *Butomus umbellatus* enlivens the edge of the pond in June.

OPPOSITE, ABOVE: *Stipa tenuissima* bursts alongside the burgeoning *Eryngium alpinum*.

OPPOSITE, BELOW: The Wet Area is also at its peak flowering in early summer. *Lythrum salicaria* 'Blush', *Campanula* 'Sarastro' and *Pimpinella major* 'Rosea' combine, with the foliage of *Cimicifuga simplex* 'James Compton' in the foreground.

Although other parts of the garden reach peak colour later in the season, there are significant contributions at this time of year from plants such as *Salvia* × *sylvestris* 'Dear Anja' and *Geranium* 'Patricia', with *Achillea* 'Credo' also coming in towards the end of the month. Their strong colouring makes them distinctly visible from anywhere in the field, enlivening the site to an extent which is out of proportion to the small amount of space given to them. Subtler, but repaying close inspection, are the flowers of *Eryngium alpinum* and graceful *Penstemon digitalis*. *Stipa tenuissima*, which for a large part of the year is full of movement but looks in all other ways inanimate, suddenly erupts into a soft efflorescence. The architecture of *Phlomis russeliana* is fully assembled and houses its yellow flowers. But the impact of foliage at this time of year should not be overlooked. Growth has suddenly burgeoned, especially at the luxuriant fringes of the site. *Datisca cannabina* has rocketed up and the character of plants such as *Veronicastrum*, *Astilboides* and *Sesleria* is established long before they come into flower.

BELOW AND OPPOSITE: Although the garden as a whole has not yet reached its peak, clusters of colour in beds such as the Wet Area and the Sporobolus Meadow, combined with a broad scattering of *Eremurus* 'Romance', are enough to enliven the whole site.

BELOW: *Eremurus* 'Romance' combining with *Amsonia hubrichtii* and *Salvia* × *sylvestris* 'Dear Anja'.

LEFT, TOP TO BOTTOM: The Wet Area greets visitors as they enter the garden.

Close-up of the planting in the Wet Area, featuring *Astilboides tabularis* and *Geranium* 'Spinners'.

Geranium 'Patricia' begins its long flowering, fringed by the grass *Sesleria autumnalis*.

Early summer work

Many gardeners are familiar with the concept of the 'Chelsea chop', an operation in which late-flowering perennials are cut back with a view to promoting bushy growth and restricting the ultimate height of the plant at flowering time. The name derives from the fact the best timing for this is thought to correspond roughly with the Chelsea Flower Show, in the latter half of May. In the Oudolf Field, this task, which some call 'pruning' of perennials, is approached with a bit more flexibility. On the whole, by early summer the window for digging up plants has drawn to a close, but pruning the plants' growth above ground can be an additional means of regulating competition. There is, for instance, a vigorous battle for above-ground supremacy in some of the 'buttress' beds between the tall asters *Aster umbellatus* and *Aster novae-angliae* 'Violetta' and the rambunctious but shorter *Persicaria amplexicaulis* 'Firedance'. By 'pruning' the asters selectively, it is possible to achieve a particularly agreeable effect later in the year, when the persicaria has enough vigour to push its flower-spikes through and above the umbrella growth of the asters. This creates a delightful contrast of colour and form, and maintains the illusion of a completely natural competition between plants.

In general the soil will still retain a decent level of moisture at this early point of the summer, so it can be a good time for planting. In cases where plants have not come through the winter in very good shape, or are struggling for any other reason, pot-grown replacements will be planted for as long as conditions remain receptive.

Persicaria amplexicaulis 'Firedance' flowers in late summer in close association with *Aster umbellatus*. This association appears to be the result of unbridled competition; however the head gardener has subtly rigged the fight in favour of the *Persicaria*, by carefully 'pruning' the shoots of the *Aster* in early summer.

High Summer

July and August are the most colourful months in the Oudolf Field. Vibrant heleniums are still on full throttle, but also many of the late-season perennials – rudbeckias, asters, persicaria, scutellaria – begin to flower. Grasses begin to assert themselves increasingly during this period, as their late season of growth approaches its climax. But even as the kaleidoscope of colours continues to turn and intensify, time begins to catch up with the Field, as petals begin to fall, seeds mature and stems harden. Maturity comes, bearing blemishes, and decay is already on the march. Many gardeners will try and avert this catastrophe for as long as possible – putting off the inevitable by assiduous dead-heading, cutting back, or bedding out with a fresh host of annuals. But in the end death arrives every year, and Oudolf's approach has long been to embrace it.

ABOVE: An *Echinacea pallida* 'Hula Dancer' seedhead in contrast with the whispy awns of *Stipa tenuissima*.

OPPOSITE, TOP: grasses become increasingly important as the year progresses. *Sporobolus heterolepis* in the foreground, with strong clumps of *Panicum virgatum* 'Shenandoah' in the background and middle distance.

OPPOSITE, BOTTOM: *Molinia caerulea* subsp. *caerulea* 'Moorhexe' and the seedheads of *Echinacea pallida* and *Stachys officinalis* 'Hummelo' add an air of maturity to the planting.

Through the advocacy of Piet and many others, the appreciation of perennials' winter skeletons has greatly increased over the last couple of decades as people become conscious of the aesthetic possibilities and wildlife benefits of leaving dead growth standing over the winter. But in midsummer, when the garden is at its peak? Oudolf's acceptance of decayed plants as part of his landscapes is uncompromising. Thus, a plant such as *Phlomis russeliana*, which traditionalists may tend to disregard due to its flowering structures turning brown too early, has been embraced by the New Perennial Movement. Its architectural quality has never been in doubt, but rather than seeing its premature senescence as a flaw, Piet's approach is to accept its decay and use it, however early in the year it may come. Brown stems and seedheads are part of his aesthetic language and their acceptance opens up a whole new range of possibilities.

Piet's plant selection is known for supplying late colour. Above left to right: *Serratula seoanei*; *Persicaria amplexicaulis* 'Orange Field' with *Succisa pratensis*; *Penstemon digitalis* 'Husker's Red' with *Panicum virgatum* 'Shenandoah'.

BELOW: *Phlomis russeliana* seedheads, brown and dry in an otherwise freshly flowering scene.

A turning point

The 'ditchside' plantings around the edges of the garden increasingly come into their own as the summer progresses. Rudbeckias, anemones, asters, persicaria and sanguisorba all jostle one another as they come into full growth and bloom, remaining resolutely verdant and colourful, with a couple of small exceptions. The spidery, veil-like inflorescence of *Aruncus* 'Horatio' has turned a pale biscuit colour, its beauty still undimmed. *Deschampsia cespitosa* 'Goldtau' has already turned brown and dry in contrast to the still burgeoning growth of other grasses such as *Panicum*, *Molinia* and *Spodiopogon*. The 'dry' Sporobolus Meadow, on the other hand, has entered its rich senescent phase – the *Sporobolus heterolepis* itself is in seed, and the petals of *Echinacea pallida* have dropped, leaving the cones hardened and black. Amid the sporobolus during this period the flowering of *Asclepias incarnata* draws to a close, and with good timing you may witness the dramatic moment when the seedpods, freshly opened, reveal the silky fruit before it takes flight. In this area only two plants, *Aster tataricus* and *Imperata cylindrica* grass, still remain fresh.

Contrasts abound at this turning point of the year.

BELOW: the 'ditchside' beds are generally in full flow. Here only *Aruncus* 'Horatio' has turned brown.

OPPOSITE, ABOVE: *Sanguisorba officinalis* 'Red Buttons' comes into its own, with *Molinia caerulea* subsp. *arundinacea* 'Transparent'.

OPPOSITE, BELOW: the Sporobolus Meadow dazzles even in its dying phase.

At this turning point of the season, there are contrasts everywhere between plants in their vegetative and senescent phases. In making plant combinations, Piet gives precedence to the strength of plant form over colour, or whether the plant tissue happens to be alive or dying. In this way the similarities of form between the inflorescences of *Eryngium yuccifolium*, the spent *Echinacea pallida* seedheads and the dark baubles of *Sanguisorba officinalis* 'Red Buttons', all inhabiting a soft hazy undergrowth, answer well to one another regardless of their freshness or lack of it.

But more than this, in allowing the presence of plants that have 'gone over' in the summer garden, the potential range of contrasts in terms of colours and textures is increased. *Scutellaria incana* comes into flower late and the freshness of its sky-blue flowers is emphasized by comparison with the straw tones of the ripening

Senescence adds to the dazzling array of contrasts, in colour, texture and density.

BELOW, CLOCKWISE FROM TOP LEFT: *Scutellaria incana* with *Sporobolus heterolepis*; senescent E*ryngium alpinum* holds its own in the foreground; the strong form of *Echinops bannaticus* amid the late-flowering umbellifer *Selinum wallichianum*; *Deschampsia cespitosa* 'Goldtau' senescent amid fresh *Eupatorium maculatum* 'Snowball', *Rudbeckia subtomentosa* and *Panicum* 'Cloud Nine'.

Luxuriant growth and flowers in the marginal 'ditchside' plantings.

TOP: *Sanguisorba officinalis* 'Blackthorn', *Veronicastrum* 'Diane', *Rudbeckia subtomentosa* and *Aster macrophyllus* 'Twilight' flower with *Vitex agnus-castus* 'Silver Spire'.

CENTRE: *Anemone hupehensis* 'Hadspen Abundance' backed by *Molinia caerulea* subsp. *arundinacea* 'Transparent'.

BOTTOM: Fresh *Aster macrophyllus* 'Twilight' combines with *Deschampsia cespitosa* 'Goldtau'.

sporobolus grass next to it. Not only does this pairing work very effectively in terms of contrasts of colour, form and texture, the act of combining a plant in full bloom with something dying enhances the fragile value of the blossom. At this time of year, when the blackbirds stop singing, it is natural to be feeling poignant about the passing of time. Piet's gardening style reflects this straightforwardly, while other garden-makers might be making huge efforts at this time of year to ward off the taint of senescence for a few more weeks.

Allowing time to wreak its effects naturally on the borders introduces a new level of dynamism to plant contrasts. Not only are there many individual examples where plants in different phases of growth are juxtaposed, but the tension between growth and decay is played out on a grand scale across the whole of the Field. The predominant senescence of the Sporobolus Meadow contrasts markedly with the freshness and vibrant colours at the verges of the site.

OPPOSITE, TOP: The solid forms of *Eryngium yuccifolium* and *Echinacea pallida* 'Hula Dancer' echo one another.

OPPOSITE, BOTTOM: The Sporobolus Meadow sits at the heart of the Oudolf Field, and contrasts with the freshness and luxuriance at the margins.

BELOW: *Thalictrum rochebruneanum* in misty light with *Deschampsia cespitosa* 'Goldtau' and *Aster macrophyllus* 'Twilight'.

High summer work

In general, high summer brings some respite from border work. The planting will have completely woven itself together to the extent that very little light reaches the soil surface to encourage the germination or growth of weeds, so they are generally held in check. Because the planting is so full and thick, moving through the beds is in any case awkward and potentially damaging. In the summer just past at the time of writing (2018), the weather was so extraordinarily hot that the gardeners had to spend an exceptional amount of time watering.

The preference is to spot-water plants individually by hand with a long lance as they need it – different plants will be tolerant of drought to varying degrees, so use of a sprinkler is too indiscriminate and wasteful. Overhead watering with a sprinkler can also lead to plants splaying and collapsing under the weight of the

ABOVE AND OPPOSITE: Lawn turf is an important component part of the design in the Oudolf Field. Grass paths intersect the borders and the grass mounds at the centre of the garden are a constant foil to the kaleidoscopic changes taking place in the garden. Summer, when the pace of working the borders slows down, provides the gardening team with a good opportunity to catch up on lawn maintenance.

As the borders fill up and knit together, weed germination decreases greatly as less and less light is allowed to reach the soil.

cascading water. Another measure to combat drought in extremis would be to cut back plants to reduce transpiration. The garden is watered exclusively with spring water; nonetheless, there's an awareness of the need to be economical.

Summer allows more time to catch up with odd jobs. Very little infrastructure was in place when the garden was first planted and compost bins, sheds and standing-out areas were added as required as was a new pump to facilitate faster irrigation of the garden. Mowing continues as normal throughout the summer and it is a good time to aerate the grass paths that serve the thousands of visitors to the garden, or to remove algae from the pond if required.

Autumn

This is traditionally a period of bounty, when the year's work reaches its culmination. Although it is perhaps not a 'season of fruitfulness' in the classic sense, growth in the borders has reached a satisfying maturity. The latent architecture of the herbaceous planting is finally fully visible, where there was nothing in the spring. 'Structural' planting is a term often reserved for woody plants, trees or shrubs that have a permanent presence, but there are only herbaceous plants here to make 'bones' and they must regrow them every year, only establishing them fully near the year's end. Although the Sporobolus Meadow at the centre of the garden will have long since reached the climax of its growth, only the autumn sees the taller-growing fringes of the site blossom. As for late-flowering herbaceous plants, their blossoming is more than just a show of colour; it is the consummation of their growth, when their full form is realized. As a composition, the Oudolf Field is at its most complete in the autumn. Whether plants are green, in colour or have long since begun to decay, their forms are still intact, and their strength underpins our enjoyment of the garden in its full glory.

TOP: The mercurial effects of light in the Sporobolus Meadow – the grass as it withers lacks substance but it gathers light in a most extraordinary way.

CENTRE: A broader view of autumn in the Oudolf Field.

BOTTOM: Late flowers persist into early autumn – here *Selinum wallichianum* flowers with *Echinacea purpurea* 'Fatal Attraction' and *Pycnanthemum muticum*.

Autumn is as dynamic as its mirror season, the spring. Both are bridges between winter and summer and see the most change between their respective beginnings and endings. The traditional view among gardeners is that spring should be the more enjoyable of these two transitions, being full of growth and promise rather than their corollary, decay, but Piet has done a lot to reverse this thinking. He chooses a high proportion of perennials, including grasses, that give of their best late in the season, but more than this, he focuses on plants that look good in their senescent phase and continue to express their character long after all life has left their super-terranean tissue. Therefore, the onset of winter may progressively reduce the colour spectrum to a series of browns as moisture retreats from stems, leaves and petals, but the structure of plant forms is a strong backbone that will long outlast the season.

However, the start of autumn is as colourful as any other time. The weather is often very good in September. We know the summer is over and do not feel the same sense of entitlement to sunshine, so every fine day offers pure enjoyment, unsullied by expectation. The nip in the air on a clear morning offers just the dash of piquancy required to quicken our appreciation of radiant warmth as the day progresses. Best of all, the sun has a much lower trajectory in the sky, and the oblique light that strikes the garden bathes it in visual warmth. The quality of light that is only available at ungodly hours on summer mornings gradually spreads throughout the day. The numerous grasses that populate the field, and in particular the sporobolus, are the perfect vehicles for that light, and seem to intensify its warmth, but all colours are improved and have a precious quality at this time of year. As flowers and leaves decay, one by one, their skeletons only intensify the gratitude we feel for those that remain. And we should not forget that the process of decay often yields a spectacular show of its own; herbaceous perennials are not as well known for autumnal leaf effects as are woody plants, but those such as *Amsonia hubrichtii* and *Aruncus* 'Horatio' offer a prolonged display of autumn leaf colour. The molinias also give their best in autumn; as they begin to decay they are much more colourful than at the transparent peak of their flowering.

Autumn is a fast-changing season of transition, featuring a patchwork of plants that decay in their own rhythm.

TOP: View across the Wet Area where *Sesleria* 'Greenlee' is still quite green. The foliage of *Darmera peltata*, to the left, however is decidedly autumnal as are the *Molinia* cultivars in the background.

CENTRE: The autumn colour that certain herbaceous plants can contribute is perhaps overlooked in general. Here *Aruncus* 'Horatio' is ablaze.

BOTTOM: The play of light is a huge factor at Hauser & Wirth Somerset, particularly in the autumn. In the absence of direct sunlight, the mood is decidedly sombre, but this can change magically in an instant.

Eventually frost will come, and if the mercury drops dramatically the garden can become considerably more monochrome overnight – but even after this, colour contrasts in the garden remain striking. Flowers are blackened easily, but the tissues of leaves and stems are considerably harder to break down and give up their colour much more slowly. Life leaves them gradually and as a result, colour still makes a dynamic, shifting contribution to the landscape throughout autumn, enhanced by the increasingly dramatic effects of the light.

BELOW, LEFT: Frost is taking an increasing toll on the landscape, but there is still plenty to admire. Note the strong resistance of *Aster tataricus* 'Jindai' and *Sedum* 'Matrona' to early autumnal frosts.

BELOW, RIGHT: Stripped bare by the cold weather, certain plants acquire an elegant economy of expression. Here *Gillenia trifoliata* and *Molinia caerulea* subsp. *caerulea* 'Moorhexe' in the contemplative setting of the Cloister Garden.

Sustained colour

To some gardeners, it is surprising how many perennials can be in flower at the commencement of autumn, when many gardens are well past their best. These are mostly present in their highest concentration in the beds at the corners and sides of the site. Some have exceptionally long seasons and although they may have been flowering since the beginning of July, they still manage to look fresh and are going strong throughout September. Such are the various Japanese anemones (*Anemone × hybrida* 'Honorine Jobert', *A. hupehensis* var. *japonica* 'Pamina', *A. hupehensis* 'Hadspen Abundance', and *A. × hybrida* 'Robustissima'), *Eupatorium maculatum*, *Persicaria amplexicaulis* cultivars and the indefatigable *Geranium* 'Rozanne'. Whereas the pale pink *Lythrum salicaria* 'Blush' has gone mostly skeletal by this time of year, its cousin *Lythrum virgatum* 'Swirl' has an unexpectedly long season in flower and is still a cloud of pink amid a sea of decaying tissue in the Sporobolus Meadow. *Selinum wallichianum*, although it is the latest umbel to flower, has already been blooming for much of the summer. It is still very noticeable late in the year, as much for its emerald green foliage as for the continuation of its flowering.

Other plants only begin to flower at summer's end or past it. The most extreme example of this is the extraordinary *Aster tataricus* 'Jindai'. Even in the unusually hot English summer of 2018, this tall daisy did not flower until October. But flowering or not, as the season progresses, it becomes increasingly noticeable for the rude health of its rather coarse green foliage. This is particularly the case in the early-dying Sporobolus Meadow, but as growth declines in general each plant of the aster becomes a beacon of good health and draws one's eye around a large part of the garden. It is always the last man standing in a haze of autumnal colour. *Aster lateriflorus* 'Horizontalis', though not quite as late as *A. tataricus*, may not come into flower until late September, at which point it becomes densely clustered with tiny daisies and eager bees. *A. umbellatus* and *A. novae-angliae* 'Violetta' are also late. Shrubs *Vitex agnus-castus* and *Indigofera amblyantha*, having been cut back to a framework in the spring, flower their hardest in September.

As a footnote, the mounds of mown grass that populate the path towards the centre of the meadow come into particularly strong relief at this time of change, remaining a vibrant green.

OPPOSITE: One of very few shrubby plants in the garden, *Vitex agnus-castus* 'Silver Spires' flowers late in the year. Every year in spring it is pruned hard back to stumps, so it stays in step with the herbaceous plants that surround it.

Structural seedheads

The sporobolus grass becomes an extraordinarily effective counterpoint at this time, not only to the stronger colours and shapes that surround it, but also to the gradually ossifying forms in its midst. *Echinacea pallida* 'Hula Dancer', which had seemed such an ethereal being when it flowered early in the summer, has become the most solid and terse expression of form imaginable. Whereas the grass gathers and plays with sunlight at this time of year more than any other, the echinaceas' hard cones deny it absolutely. There is no doubt that the sea of sporobolus at the heart of the meadow enhances our appreciation of solid forms as they develop throughout the garden. *Phlomis russeliana*, echinops and heleniums all begin to answer one another as they shed the adornment of colour and soft tissue. The garden is all about form, transparency and solidity now.

ABOVE, LEFT TO RIGHT: The looming form of *Datisca cannabina* has a strong presence throughout its season of growth. Now gaunt, it is no less imposing; *Aster amellus* 'Sonora' – its seedheads show good persistence and catch what light there is as winter approaches; the contrasting seedheads of *Thalictrum rochebruneanum* and *Deschampsia cespitosa* 'Goldtau'.

TOP: The terse solidity of echinacea 'cones' in a sea of hazy *Sporobolus heterolepis*, with the ethereal spikes of *Persicaria amplexicaulis* 'Alba' in the background.

CENTRE: Autumn foliage colour in the foreground from *Amsonia hubrichtii*. *Eryngium yuccifolium* seedheads mimic those of *Echinacea pallida*.

BOTTOM: Autumn light plays on *Aruncus* 'Horatio', the seedheads casting a delicately sombre veil over the flame-coloured autumn foliage.

OPPOSITE: The apparatus of flowers often gains more structural importance once it is stripped of the ephemeral – here the seedheads of *Phlomis russeliana* stand out much more than its flowers did.

LEFT, ABOVE: Autumnal *Echinacea* and *Sporobolus*. This is a combination that evolves throughout the seasons, arguably at its most effective when both plants are pared back to the essential elements of their form.

LEFT, BELOW: The grass *Bouteloua curtipendula* in flower.

Grasses

A number of the grasses have been prominent for some time. Although *Sesleria autumnalis* is now flowering, the foliage is still its most prominent feature. It is remarkable for its constancy from season to season, but with its faint chartreuse tinge, its freshness becomes ever more prominent as autumn progresses. It makes a startling colour contrast with the deep burgundy *Sedum* 'Matrona' in the Field, whereas in the Cloister it interacts much more subtly with the shifting colours of *Molinia caerulea* subsp. *caerulea* 'Moorhexe'. By contrast, *Sporobolus heterolepis* undergoes a considerable transformation during this season. The weight of its flowering and seeding parts in August makes the stalks pendent, to the extent that their tips are almost grazing the ground, and the whole Sporobolus Meadow at that time becomes rather a formless, conjoined haze. As the plant ripens and dries, it loses weight and assumes a successively more upright, individual form. From then on, the plant gradually loses colour until it is quite bleached, and its silhouette exerts an ever finer tracery on its surroundings. It is a prime example of how rich and dynamic the processes of ripening, senescence and death can be in the garden.

BELOW: In close detail, *Sporobolus heterolepis* etches its fine tracery throughout the Sporobolus Meadow, shown here with the seedheads of *Dianthus carthusianorum*.

OPPOSITE, ABOVE: *Sesleria autumnalis* holds its chartreuse-tinged freshness later than most grasses.

OPPOSITE, BELOW: *Molinia caerulea* subsp. *caerulea* 'Edith Dudszus' in flower before frost has pared it back, wreaking a remarkable transformation on the character of the plant.

The switch grasses (*Panicum* species) are reasonably inconspicuous for much of the year, although their foliage is quite voluminous. However, they flower hazily at a great height in late summer and autumn. *P. virgatum* 'Cloud Nine' is a giant, as tall as anything in the garden once in full flow; *P. virgatum* 'Shenandoah', although much shorter, assumes prominence by colouring a rich crimson at its tips at this time of year. Reed-like *Spodiopogon sibiricus*, so late into growth, now becomes dominant, especially where it is planted extensively in the Magnolia Bed in the farmyard. *Pennisetum alopecuroides* f. *viridescens* continues to flower without much degradation for much of autumn. But perhaps of all grasses the season belongs chiefly to the molinias, which now add colour to their remarkable grace of form. The basal foliage colours up spectacularly, but long after this has perished the warm tones of the flowering structure remain. In a somewhat similar manner to the sporobolus, the form of the grass benefits from desiccation, with its clean, flowing lines in full evidence without the obstruction of the leaf-clump.

BELOW, LEFT: *Spodiopogon sibiricus* flowering late in the year.

BELOW, RIGHT: *Panicum virgatum* 'Shenandoah' subtly develops agreeable russet tones that befit the season well. Here it forms a decorative fringe to the globular forms of *Echinops bannaticus*.

Autumn work

In many gardens, the arrival of the first frosts would signal time on the year's display, and borders would begin to be dismantled as the focus turned to the following year but here the plants stand untouched all winter. Nevertheless, as foliage desiccates, thins and falls, pockets of soil around the plants open up again and allow limited access to the borders. Because the window of opportunity for lifting and splitting plants is limited to a short time in spring, autumn brings an early chance to do some advance tasks, so that spring work is as streamlined as possible. This means autumn is largely dedicated to weeding, including selectively thinning out seedlings of those

ABOVE AND OPPOSITE: Although the beds still look full, as frost dessicates foliage, the texture of the planting becomes much more open again. This both encourages germination and permits access to the garden team to start weeding again. Work must be undertaken with some care in order not to disturb the effect of standing perennials which must be preserved throughout winter. However, if all were left until the spring, when everything is cut down, there would be far too much to do in one season.

plants with a propensity to self-sow; *Dianthus carthusianorum* is one of the worst offenders, as there are plentiful opportunities for it to colonize the open sward of the Sporobolus Meadow. Nevertheless, care has to be taken with this task to ensure that there are enough seedlings left to allow a good succession of this short-lived species. Some other plants self-sow more mildly, and the head gardener may seize upon these opportunities to propagate his stock – he has found it useful to lift seedlings of *Asclepias incarnata* and grow them on in a pot, before slotting them back into the garden the following year.

Plant Directory

The planting at Hauser & Wirth Somerset has been remarkably stable since its installation. For this reason, the plant directory below mimics almost exactly Piet's original plant list, with very few additions. A list of selected bulbs used in the project is included at the end in a separate section.

A note on plant names

A number of important changes to plant nomenclature have occurred since Piet created his planting plans for the garden. The most seismic of these is that the genus *Aster* has been split and many of its species are now reassigned to new genera. In order to maintain consistency with the original planting plan, this book has adhered to the names used by Piet at that time. However, the updated names are included in brackets in the headings for each relevant entry in the plant directory.

Hardiness ratings

The hardiness of each plant in the directory is denoted according to the Royal Horticultural Society's system.

Royal
Horticultural
Society

RHS Hardiness Ratings

RHS rating	Temperature ranges (°C)	Category	Definition	USDA rating
H1a	>15	Heated greenhouse – tropical	Under glass all year	13
H1b	10–15	Heated greenhouse – subtropical	Can be grown outside in the summer in hotter, sunny and sheltered locations (such as city centre areas), but generally perform better under glass	12
H1c	5–10	Heated greenhouse – warm temperate	Can be grown outside in the summer throughout most of the UK while day-time temperatures are high enough to promote growth. (Most bedding plants, tomatoes and cucumbers.)	11
H2	1–5	Tender – cool or frost-free greenhouse	Tolerant of low temperatures, but not surviving being frozen. Except in frost-free inner-city areas on coastal extremities requires glasshouse conditions. Can be grown outside once risk of frost is over. (Most succulents, many subtropical plants, annual bedding plants, many spring-sown vegetables.)	10b
H3	1– -5	Half hardy – unheated greenhouse/ mild winter	Hardy in coastal and relatively mild parts of the UK except in severe winters and at risk from sudden (early) frosts. May be hardy elsewhere with wall shelter or good microclimate. Likely to be damaged or killed in cold winters, particularly with no snow cover or if pot grown. Can often survive with some artificial protection in winter. (Many Mediterranean-climate plants, spring-sown vegetables for later harvesting.)	9b/10a
H4	-10 – -5	Hardy – average winter	Hardy through most of the UK apart from inland valleys, at altitude, and central/northerly locations. May suffer foliage damage and stem dieback in harsh winters in cold gardens. Some normally hardy plants may not survive long wet winters in heavy or poorly drained soil. Plants in pots are more vulnerable to harsh winters, particularly evergreens and many bulbs. (Many herbaceous and woody plants, winter brassicas, leeks).	8b/9a
H5	-15 – -10	Hardy – cold winter	Hardy in most places throughout the UK even in severe winters. May not withstand open/exposed sites or central/northern locations. Many evergreens will suffer foliage damage, and plants in pots will be at increased risk. (Many herbaceous and woody plants, some brassicas, leeks.)	7b/8a
H6	-20 – -15	Hardy – very cold winter	Hardy in all of UK and northern Europe. Many plants grown in containers will be damaged unless given protection. (Herbaceous and woody plants from continental climates.)	6b/7a
H7	< -20	Very hardy	Hardy in the severest European continental climates including exposed upland locations in the UK. (Herbaceous and woody plants from continental climates.)	6a–1

Note
The R.H.S. temperature ranges are intended to be absolute minimum temperatures (°C), not the long-term average annual extreme minimum temperature used for the USDA zone ratings.

Reproduced with kind permission of the Royal Horticultural Society. For more information, visit rhs.org.uk/hardiness-rating.

ACHILLEA 'CREDO'
One of the more strapping achilleas, though not always long-lived, this is a prominent feature of the Oudolf Field in July. Its flowers, arranged in the shape of a dome, offer a good structural contrast with the strongly upright salvias. The flower colour, although bright, is of the soothing variety of yellow, washed with cream to varying degrees dependent on the maturity of the inflorescence. The spent flowers become pleasantly bleached as the summer progresses, with the structural presence of the plant undiminished.
Height: 1m (3¼ft) *Hardiness*: H7
Soil: Good drainage is required
Exposure: Full sun

ACHILLEA 'FEUERLAND'
This achillea has been something of a disappointment in the Oudolf Field. The head gardener often bemoans the unreliable nature of achilleas in general and finds that as a tribe, they are inclined to die at a moment's notice. To compound matters, 'Feuerland' in particular, due to some inherent malady, has never successfully opened its flowers in the Oudolf Field. Later flowering than 'Credo', and of a less domineering stature, it would have filled a niche in the light-textured Sporobolus Meadow. However, at the time of writing it looks destined for the chop.
Height: 70cm (2⅓ft) *Hardiness*: H7
Soil: Good drainage is required
Exposure: Full sun

ACHILLEA 'HELLA GLASHOFF'
This is a fairly robust perennial with a long flowering season, persisting well into early autumn. Flowers open a lemon yellow,

OPPOSITE, LEFT
Achillea 'Credo'

OPPOSITE, RIGHT
Achillea 'Hella Glashoff'

BELOW, LEFT
Agastache foeniculum in late summer

BELOW, RIGHT
Allium 'Summer Beauty'

fading to creamy off-white as they slowly age.
Height: 50cm (20in) *Hardiness*: H7
Soil: Good drainage is required
Exposure: Full sun

AGASTACHE FOENICULUM

Agastache is a genus with no discernible weakness save for the fact that slow early growth can sometimes lead to the plant being swamped by early risers in the spring, or devoured by slugs before it can get going. Its architecture is a classic expression of opposite growth, and from midsummer onwards the plant is adorned like a candelabra with perfectly erect inflorescences. The clear blue flowers of *A. foeniculum* are much frequented by bees. As is common in the mint family, the calyces have a fuzzy presence all of their own which outlasts the long flowering season and persists well into the cold months.
Height: 1m (3¼ft) *Hardiness*: H4
Soil: Good drainage is helpful in winter *Exposure*: Full sun

ALLIUM 'SUMMER BEAUTY'

Somewhat atypically a clump-forming allium, making a mat of lustrous green leaves which is quite prominent from early spring onwards, this plant offers an attractive foil for spring-flowering bulbs. The flowers are produced over a long period in summer and look like giant chives. It is not perhaps as attention-grabbing as some of the earlier-flowering allium cultivars, but it offers a good deal in terms of longevity and foliage contribution.
Height: 60cm (2ft) *Hardiness*: H6
Soil: Not fussy as long as not waterlogged *Exposure*: Full sun

ALLIUM TUBEROSUM

As with *A.* 'Summer Beauty',
although it is technically bulbous,
this behaves like a normal clump-
forming herbaceous plant and does
not undergo dormancy in summer.
Known as Chinese chives, it has
edible leaves but the plant is a
much statelier one than the flimsy
European version. The flowerhead
is hemispherical rather than
perfectly round and held at a
generous height above the
ground-hugging clump of foliage.
In the Oudolf Field it makes a
good flowering companion to
Scutellaria incana.
Height: 60cm (2ft)   *Hardiness*: H5
Soil: Moist but well-drained
Exposure: Full sun

AMORPHA CANESCENS

An extraordinary little plant,
A. canescens looks utterly dead in
winter and early spring when all it
manages to present to the world
above ground is a couple of
forlorn-looking twigs about 30cm
(12in) high. However, it comes
alive in what seems a miraculous
fashion, furnishing itself with very
neat and characterful grey-green
leaves. The flower spikes are
predominantly lavender in colour,
but with bright orange stamens. Its
common name of 'lead plant' refers
to the belief held by American
settlers that its presence indicated
lead in the soil.
Height: 90cm (3ft)   *Hardiness*: H7
Soil: Drought-tolerant and
presumably averse to winter wet
Exposure: Full sun

AMSONIA HUBRICHTII

A. hubrichtii is perhaps not seen as
often as other members of its
genus, although it is quite the most

striking. This is probably because it is rather slow to get going and multiply – the nurseries that grow it always seem to be short of stock. Once it is established, you have a plant of almost shrub-like solidity and stature. The pale blue flowers offer very effective early season colour but do not come high on the plant's list of virtues because of its excellence in other departments. The needle-like foliage presents a soft, swaying haze and the autumn colour, a rich, buttery yellow, is perhaps the most sustained and striking display of any herbaceous plant. The winter skeleton is gaunt, but noticeably silver. Such subtle variations of tone and colouring are a treasured part of the winter scene at the garden.
Height: 60–90cm (2–3ft) *Hardiness*: H5 *Soil*: Not fussy *Exposure*: Sun/ light shade

ANEMONE HUPEHENSIS 'HADSPEN ABUNDANCE'

This anemone is quite like 'Pamina' (below) in that it is a similar height and the flowers are a dark saturated pink. But this is a single-flowered clone that has an interesting irregularity in its corolla, in that alternate petals are either dark and slightly shorter, or pale and slightly longer, creating a charming variegated effect. The central boss of golden stamens is a strong feature.
Height: 1m (3¼ft) *Hardiness*: H7 *Soil*: Tolerant of all sorts, but happiest in moisture-retentive, rich soil *Exposure*: Tolerant of light shade, but happiest in sun

ANEMONE HUPEHENSIS VAR. JAPONICA 'PAMINA'

'Pamina' shares many of the excellent qualities of 'Honorine Jobert', although it may not be

quite as long in flower. It fills a slightly different niche in the garden as it is shorter and its semi-double flowers are a full-blooded pink. As a bonus it retains its feathery seeds for longer than other varieties, and these are unexpected beacons of gathered light in the winter.
Height: 1m (3¼ft) *Hardiness*: H7
Soil: Tolerant of all sorts, but happiest in moisture-retentive, rich soil *Exposure*: Tolerant of light shade, but prefers sun

ANEMONE X HYBRIDA 'HONORINE JOBERT'
It seems almost superfluous to describe the virtues of such a long-established and well-known garden plant. Its flowering performance is unimpeachable – exceptionally long (it is capable of flowering from early summer until the frosts, with no dead-heading), with a clean petal-drop. However, for a plant of considerable presence in growth it offers comparatively little in the winter.
Height: 1.4–1.6m (4½–5¼ft)
Hardiness: H7 *Soil*: Tolerant of all sorts of conditions, but happiest in moisture-retentive, rich soil
Exposure: Tolerant of light shade, but prefers to be positioned in an open site in full sun

ANEMONE X HYBRIDA 'ROBUSTISSIMA'
A lovely clear pink, single-flowered Japanese anemone, similar in stature to 'Honorine Jobert', but rather later into flower, starting in mid to late summer and lasting well into the autumn. It holds its own against its neighbours in the corner beds closest to the pavilion.
Height: 1.3–1.5m (4¼–5ft)
Hardiness: H7 *Soil*: Tolerant of all sorts, but happiest in moisture-

LEFT
Anemone x hybrida 'Robustissima'
RIGHT
Aquilegia vulgaris in bud

retentive, rich soil *Exposure*: Tolerant of light shade, but prefers an open site in full sun

ANEMONE RIVULARIS

Its Latin name translates as 'windflower of riverbanks' and it does seem a child of nature. The flashy reverse side of the petals is riven with a beautifully rich, cool violet colour. The open side of the flower shows pure white petals, but the stamens repeat the violet colouring to charming effect. As with many herbaceous anemones, it will run at the root somewhat. It doesn't have the longevity in flower, nor stature, of 'Honorine Jobert' but it has an abundance of natural charm. This plant was used to replace *Anemone* 'Wild Swan', which was reluctant to grow. *Height*: 1m (3¼ft) *Hardiness*: H5 *Soil*: Tolerant of all sorts, but happiest in moisture-retentive, rich soil *Exposure*: Tolerant of light shade, but prefers sun

AQUILEGIA VULGARIS

This was an opportunistic arrival, an interloper that presumably arrived as seed in the potting soil of nursery-grown stock. Nevertheless, it is tolerated in the field, and offers useful early growth and colour in a planting which peaks much later. A profuse seeder, its will to colonize must be carefully controlled, as it is much more competitive in spring than many of the late-flowering perennials will tolerate. If it is chopped right to the ground as the flowers fade it will respond with a fresh crop of slightly glaucous foliage.
Height: 80cm (2¾ft) *Hardiness*: H7 *Soil*: Enjoys moist soil. *Exposure*: Full sun or partial shade

ARUNCUS 'HORATIO'

This aruncus is a hybrid between
A. dioicus and *A. aethusifolius*. This
grafts some of the fine-textured
quality of the latter onto a larger
plant, although the vigour of
'Horatio' doesn't quite match that
of the rambunctious *A. dioicus*. As
well as finer leaves, this hybrid
features lovely, spidery, weeping
flower heads. Strictly speaking, the
flowering season is incredibly short
– the blooms may not remain
white for quite two weeks – but
when they decay to a biscuit
colour they are barely less
appealing, and they remain in this
state for a good few months,
creating a warm, transparent veil.
The cross was made by Ernst
Pagels, one of a number of
continental nurserymen who
helped to mould the New
Perennial Movement by growing
and breeding perennials suitable for
use in naturalistic planting schemes.
Height: 1.2m (4ft) *Hardiness*: H6
Soil: Loves moisture *Exposure*: Full
sun or partial shade.

ASCLEPIAS INCARNATA

The swamp milkweed is native to
wetlands over much of the USA
and is prized there by conserva-
tionists as it is the preferred food of
monarch butterfly larvae. Its
scented rosy-budded flowers are
attractive enough, but the real
show comes from the seedheads.
Pointing dramatically upwards, they
split to reveal an interior packed
with the silky down of the seeds.
Once these have flown the pods
remain an object of interest for the
rest of the year.
Height: 1.8m (6ft) *Hardiness*: H7
Soil: Needs moisture and tolerates a
heavy soil. *Exposure*: Full sun.

ASTER AMELLUS 'SONORA'

Ostensibly similar to *Aster macrophyllus* 'Twilight' in that it is a shortish purple daisy, 'Sonora' is much more compact, stiff and solid in its growth. In flower, though, it comes to life, with a stronger, more stimulating colour than 'Twilight' – a definite violet-purple which contrasts vibrantly with the central boss of golden stamens. Standard for an aster, you may think, but in this case the contrast is particularly effective. The species from which this cultivar derives is from Central and Southern Europe (it is named for a tributary of the Po) and is said to be more drought-tolerant than many asters.

Height: 60cm (2ft) *Hardiness*: H7
Soil: Not fussy *Exposure*: Full sun or partial shade

ASTER LATERIFLORUS 'HORIZONTALIS'

(now *Symphyotrichum lateriflorum* var. *horizontale*)
An unusual aster in that it offers more in terms of structure than pure floral contribution. It has dense growth and very small leaves and a painstaking build-up to flowering in mid to late autumn. It emerges from a very small crown of basal leaves and gradually, through the course of a year, establishes a rigid framework of branches that spread laterally way beyond their point of origin. A row of it in mature growth appears like a dark hedge with purple-tinted foliage. Apart from this there is absolutely no colour until very late, when each plant suddenly becomes smothered in tiny reddish daisies.

Height: 70cm (2¼ft) *Hardiness*: H7
Soil: Not fussy *Exposure*: Happiest in full sun

ASTER 'LITTLE CARLOW' (NOW SYMPHYOTRICHUM 'LITTLE CARLOW')

This aster is a well-established, trouble-free hybrid between *A. cordifolius* and *A. novi-belgii*. Robust and unassuming in its growth phase, it produces billowing clouds of small daisies with soft lilac rays and yellow cones – a pleasant effect that tends to enhance other colours around it. The flowering period is late and long, lasting throughout early and mid autumn. The minuscule leaves are dark and narrow, on strong, wiry stems. *Height*: 1m (3¼ft) *Hardiness*: H7 *Soil*: Not fussy *Exposure*: Happiest in full sun

ASTER MACROPHYLLUS 'TWILIGHT' (NOW EURYBIA X HERVEYI)

'Twilight' is a tough plant which is adaptable to a range of conditions, lending itself in particular to extensive woodland plantings in dappled shade. In border conditions at this partiular site it makes itself at home by spreading underground to invade its neighbours. Its flowering is very typical of the genus, with pale mauve daisies appearing from late summer to autumn. However, its appearance in early spring is also attractive and valuable, forming as it does a neat, ground-hugging mat of leaves early in the season. This spring foliage interacts intriguingly with sunlight. Another bonus is that the plant is mercifully free of mildew. *Height*: 90cm (3ft) *Hardiness*: H7 *Soil*: Not fussy *Exposure*: Full sun or partial shade

ASTER TATARICUS 'JINDAI'

This is a comparatively compact form of the species which is less

prone to keel over. It was discovered by Rich Darke and Skip March at the Jindai Botanic Gardens near Tokyo. Even in its compact form, it is imposing enough to act as a sentinel plant, especially in the late season when it reaches its full height. Its leaves are as voluminous and healthy-looking as any cabbage, but glossier. Like the burdock that grows wild in neighbouring verges, it remains resolutely green when every other plant that surrounds it has turned colour. This is particularly noticeable in the autumn, when practically every other plant has decayed – this plant remains in rude good health and is one of the last to come into flower, from mid autumn.

Height: 120-140cm (4-4½ft)
Hardiness: H7   *Soil*: Not fussy
Exposure: Happiest in full sun

ASTER UMBELLATUS (NOW *DOELLINGERIA UMBELLATA*)

A vigorous presence at the fringes of the Oudolf Field, this aster is also an important component of the planting matrix with *Spodiopogon sibiricus* and *Aster macrophyllus* 'Twilight' at the entrance to the gallery. The specific name hints at the dome-like disposition of its flowers, which make an interesting counterpoint to the taller *Eupatorium maculatum*. The head gardener likes to manipulate its eventual flowering height by 'pruning' it in late spring. It is disease-resistant, with a very long flowering season during which it is popular with a variety of pollinating insects.

Height: 1.75m (6ft) *Hardiness*: H6
Soil: Likes moisture *Exposure*: Happiest in full sun but has a degree of shade tolerance

ASTER NOVAE-ANGLIAE 'VIOLETTA' (NOW SYMPHYOTRICHUM NOVAE-ANGLIAE 'VIOLETTA')

Stiff, tall and opaque, this New England Aster could really only work in the thicker 'buttress' plantings at the corners and edges of the Oudolf Field. Here it can jostle effectively with the likes of *Datisca cannabina* and shore up the boundaries of the site. The colour, as implied, is a particularly strong, saturated violet which suffuses the numerous narrow ray florets.

It flowers in early and mid autumn and has good mildew resistance. Like all the plants in the garden, it manages to stand well without the need for staking, given full sun and exposure.

Height: 1.5–2m (5–6½ft) *Hardiness*: H7 *Soil*: Likes reasonable moisture *Exposure*: Happiest in an open site in full sun

ASTILBOIDES TABULARIS

Mainly a dweller of wet, shady and sheltered places, this plant has large but delicate-looking platform leaves that look ready to be shredded by the slightest wind. This is really an overgrown woodland saxifrage, with tall, drooping panicles of frothy white flowers. What you cannot offer in terms of shelter and light shade you must be prepared to make up for with plentiful moisture. Unsurprisingly, it features in the Wet Area of the Oudolf Field with other moisture-loving plants as companions. Although the flowers are short-lived, the plant retains its strong personality throughout the growing season.

Height: 1.5m (5ft) *Hardiness*: H6 *Soil*: Must be moist *Exposure*: Happiest in partial shade and a sheltered position

ASTRANTIA MAJOR 'ROMA'

Astrantias, with their fresh, natural charm, have long been championed by the likes of Margery Fish and Beth Chatto in this country. Their major weakness as garden plants is that they may collapse ungracefully soon after flowering and if they are planted in significant quantity this can have a negative impact later in the season (often as early as midsummer). There are numerous different cultivars of *A. major* with a range from white to burgundy. 'Roma' is a delightful faded pink and has better persistence than most other varieties.

Height: 60cm (2ft) *Hardiness*: H7 *Soil*: Must be moist *Exposure*: Full sun or partial shade

ASTRANTIA MAJOR 'VENICE'

A darker variety than 'Roma', 'Venice' is plum-coloured. It is planted in the select company of the Cloister Garden where it suits the light shade and 'woodland' atmosphere.

Height: 60cm (2ft) *Hardiness*: H7 *Soil*: Must be moist *Exposure*: Full sun or partial shade

BAPTISIA 'PURPLE SMOKE'

Baptisias can be fairly slow to establish and are difficult to move, being tap-rooted. Perhaps for these reasons they are not as popular as they deserve to be. 'Purple Smoke' arose as a chance hybrid between *Baptisia australis* and *B. alba*. It inherited the dark grey flower stems of the latter, which contributes strongly to the 'smoky' effect of this hybrid. Baptisias are often compared to lupins, but overall they are a longer-term, more rewarding investment, without the tawdry collapse of lupins, and with

a great deal more airy grace.
Height: 90cm (3ft) *Hardiness*: H7
Soil: Good drainage essential.
Exposure: Full sun

BOUTELOUA CURTIPENDULA

A fine, airy grass with a very light touch, this is one of the latest plants into growth at the garden and once it does get going it is so transparent as to be barely visible. A distinctive feature of the genus is that the flowers hang exclusively on one side of the arching stems. The plant is extremely tolerant of drought and cold.
Height: 90cm (3ft) *Hardiness*: H7
Soil: Good drainage essential.
Exposure: Full sun.

BROUSSONETIA PAPYRIFERA

This is a rarely seen tree of dubious hardiness, although the multi-stemmed specimens at the garden survived the reasonably harsh winter of 2017-18 without any problem. They benefit from the shelter and warmth afforded by the gallery buildings that surround the Cloister Garden. A quietly interesting tree with felty leaves, *B. papyrifera* is heteroblastic, meaning that the juvenile foliage has a different form to the mature leaves. Although the trees at Hauser & Wirth Somerset are mature, with oval, entire leaves, the phenomenon can still be observed when the trees send up new shoots from the base, for on these the foliage is deeply lobed. They are characterful trees which are very important structural elements of the Cloister Garden planting.
Height: 4–8m (13–26ft) *Hardiness*: H5 *Soil*: Good drainage *Exposure*: Full sun, but sheltered from cold, drying winds

BUTOMUS UMBELLATUS

The 'flowering rush' is not a rush in the botanical sense, although it could be mistaken for such until its stunning flowers make their appearance in early summer. A marginal aquatic, it produces umbels of clear pink flowers that rise to 1.2m (4ft) on leafless stems. *Height*: 1.2m (4ft) *Hardiness*: H5 *Soil*: Submerged in shallow water, any soil *Exposure*: Full sun

CALAMINTHA NEPETA SUBSP. NEPETA

A somewhat scruffy-looking but deeply appreciated perennial herb with pungently aromatic leaves, this bears its tiny flowers in a hazy cloud throughout summer and until the frost comes. Thereafter it maintains a textural presence of dark, wiry stems. This subspecies of *Calamintha* does not self-sow, unlike other members of the genus which pop up in paving cracks, walls and other places where drainage is sharp and the competition from other plants reduced. Its flowers are off-white with a tinge of lilac. *Height*: 30cm (12in) *Hardiness*: H5 *Soil*: Good drainage essential *Exposure*: Full sun

CALTHA PALUSTRIS

One of a number of marginal, pond-dwelling perennials that brighten up early spring in the Oudolf Field at this Somerset garden. *C. palustris* produces flowers that are basically buttercups, but the very largest you can find (their common name is appropriately 'kingcups'). The foliage also makes a solid contribution to the Wet Area through a large part of the year. *Height*: 30cm (12in) *Hardiness*: H7 *Soil*: Must have wet feet at all times *Exposure*: Full sun

CAMPANULA 'SARASTRO'
A very showy campanula which flowers in early to midsummer, 'Sarastro' has large, pendent flowers of a deeply saturated dark blue which in the Wet Area combines nicely with the pink umbellifer *Pimpinella major* and *Geranium* 'Spinners'. It is a sterile hybrid between *Campanula punctata* and the nettle-leaved bellflower *C. trachelium*, raised at the eponymous nursery in Austria.
Height: 70cm (2¼ft) *Hardiness*: H7
Soil: Enjoys moisture *Exposure*: Full sun or light shade

CHAEROPHYLLUM HIRSUTUM 'ROSEUM'
A British native umbellifer, it has inherited all the simple charm of a wildflower as well as the wilful self-sowing habits. This plant gets going early in the season and is in full flower when the prairie perennials at have barely started growing. With its height it is therefore a useful complement to predominantly late season plantings. Rather than hibernating, it aestivates, meaning it is dormant during the summer. As the flowers begin to fade, the whole plant can be cut to the ground without detriment, which will inhibit its invasive tendencies; it will reappear the following spring.

Height: 1m (3¼ft) *Hardiness*: H7
Soil: Enjoys moisture *Exposure*: Full sun or light shade

CIMICIFUGA SIMPLEX 'BRUNETTE', 'JAMES COMPTON' (NOW ACTAEA SIMPLEX)
An elegant pair of dark-leaved cultivars. The foliage is quite a treat in itself, with its expansively divided leaves gradually increasing in volume until a wand-like inflorescence appears at the summit

LEFT
Cimicifuga simplex 'James Compton'
RIGHT
Cimicifuga simplex 'Pritchard's Giant'

of the plant in late summer to early autumn. Every part of the plant, including the closed flower buds, which decorate the stem like baubles, is a moody maroon colour, but the flowers themselves are brilliant bursts of white. As an unexpected treat, they carry a sweet scent. 'Pritchard's Giant' is a green-leaved cultivar of the species, grown at the fringes of the site.
Height: 2m (6½ft) *Hardiness*: H7

Soil: Enjoys moisture *Exposure*: Full sun or light shade

CLEMATIS HERACLEIFOLIA 'CHINA PURPLE'

This is a herbaceous (strictly speaking 'sub-shrubby'), non-climbing species of clematis that dies back to just above ground level every winter. It bears fragrant purple flowers in late summer and autumn. It struggled to establish

and is no longer present in the Cloister Garden (snails may be to blame), but at the time of writing is just beginning to get going in the Wet Area planting.
Height: 1m (3¼ft) *Hardiness*: H6
Soil: Moist, but well-drained
Exposure: Full sun

CRAMBE CORDIFOLIA

A close relative of sea kale from the Caucasus, *C. cordifolia* is much larger

and somewhat coarser in all its parts. Quite early in the season, it produces a colossal cloud of small white cruciform flowers which are strongly scented of honey. There are few herbaceous plants with quite this sort of presence in flower. The dry wreckage of the flower structure remains recognizable for some time after the flowers have fallen. The huge leathery leaves need protection from slugs on

emergence, and later in the year from the cabbage white moth. Perhaps these pests have done for it in the Oudolf Field, where it is no longer present.
Height: 2m (6½ft) *Hardiness*: H5 *Soil*: Appreciates good drainage *Exposure*: Full sun

DARMERA PELTATA
The foliage of this plant is a very strong structural presence in summer. The stature of the plant appears to vary according to the clone and Piet has a plant whose leaves have not surpassed 25cm in 30 years. Some plants are capable of hoisting the round, scalloped leaves to a height of 1.5m (5ft), though it is such a sappy grower that it collapses to nothing after a brief colouring in autumn. The flowers are a considerable bonus, appearing before the leaves at bluebell time. *Height*: 1–1.5m (3¼–5ft) *Hardiness*: H6 *Soil*: Must be moist at all times *Exposure*: Sun or partial shade

DATISCA CANNABINA
This is a great, hulking plant, as imposing as a herbaceous species can be. It arises with real intent, at first pushing out its jagged-edged compound leaves on upright stems. As the flowers develop later in the season into long pendent tassles the stems begin to arch over from a great height and the plant becomes truly menacing. It provides a distinctive winter silhouette.
Height: 2m (6½ft) *Hardiness*: H4 *Soil*: Likes to have moisture available *Exposure*: Sun or partial shade

DESCHAMPSIA CESPITOSA 'GOLDTAU'
A low-growing evergreen tuft of basal leaves persists throughout the

ABOVE LEFT
Datisca cannabina in flower

ABOVE RIGHT
The flowery veil of *Deschampsia cespitosa*
'Goldtau' in the cloiser

BELOW
Dianthus carthusianorum

year, but in early summer the flowering stems arise to create an incredibly soft, shimmering veil. Senescence comes early to this grass, and as midsummer turns to late the flower structure is entirely sere. Its bronzy-gold colour is enhanced by sunlight, the more so as the season progresses and sunlight becomes more oblique and warm in tone. With *Sporobolus heterolepis* it is one of the best vehicles for light and a great contrast to *Molinia* cultivars.
Height: 60-80cm (2-2½ft) *Hardiness*: H6 *Soil*: Tolerates poor drainage *Exposure*: Sun or partial shade

DIANTHUS CARTHUSIANORUM

This is delightfully robust plant, considering its appearance, for it has some of the qualities of an alpine/xerophyte about it. There is that thrifty paucity of leaves topped with flowers that are disproportionate in their impact. The flower stems are so wiry, and the flowers so saturated in colour, that they often appear to be floating in mid-air, yet the plant can compete in border conditions and will proliferate by self-sowing. Perhaps not surprisingly for a plant that carries so little water in its tissue, it stands well into the winter, and is recognizably itself long after all colour and life has faded.
Height: 60cm (2ft) *Hardiness*: H6 *Soil*: Well-drained *Exposure*: Full sun

DORYCNIUM HIRSUTUM

A sub-shrubby clover relative with a lax habit and fine hairs all over its leaves, *D. hirsutum* looks as though it belongs to a warmer climate than a field in Somerset could provide, but given good drainage it is a reasonably robust plant. Once it

starts flowering in summer it does not stop until the weather turns cold. Restricted by intense sunlight and drought in its native habitat, like many garrigue-based sub-shrubs brought to our moist fertile soils it performs profligately for a couple of years and then turns quickly into a tawdry mess. It needs to be replaced when it reaches this point as it will not tolerate a hard cut-back. The

gardeners have in fact lost patience with this plant and decided to replace it with *Artemisia ludoviciana*. *Height*: 50cm (20in) *Hardiness*: H4 *Soil*: Well-drained *Exposure*: Full sun

ECHINACEA PALLIDA 'HULA DANCER'
Echinacea as a genus has a reputation for being somewhat unreliable, but Piet reckons that *E. pallida* is a very long-lived perennial. 'Hula Dancer' has

spidery pale pink ray florets which droop pleasingly, with the whole effect being rather ethereal. In midsummer these flowers float airily through the Sporobolus Meadow. When the ray florets drop, the remaining solid cones make an important contribution for the rest of the year, articulating the otherwise diaphanous haze of the matrix with a host of solid, light-absorbing dots.

Height: 1.2m (4ft) *Hardiness*: H5 *Soil*: Well-drained *Exposure*: Full sun

ECHINACEA PURPUREA 'FATAL ATTRACTION'
This plant is much more full-blooded in colouring and bearing than *E. pallida*, with rich pink flowers that are enhanced by the dark stems that carry them. The ray florets are also arranged much

more stiffly and conventionally than those of its pale and interesting cousin. It is a clone selected by Piet from his own garden at Hummelo.

Height: 1m (3ft) *Hardiness*: H5 *Soil*: Well-drained *Exposure*: Full sun

ECHINOPS BANNATICUS

E. bannaticus is an archetypal Oudolf plant, in the sense that its form and durability as a silhouette are perhaps of more value than its flowering performance. If you like neat plants that remain fresh over a long period, then this is not the plant for you. The flowering performance is brief and shortly after it the plant starts to become ragged, with the leaves gradually dying off from the base of the plant. Embrace senescence and you will value this plant for the unmistakable character of its form.

Height: 1.2m (4ft) *Hardiness*: H7 *Soil*: Well-drained *Exposure*: Full sun

ERYNGIUM ALPINUM

One of a host of blue *Eryngium* species and cultivars available, it probably has the largest inflorescence when you take into account the gorgeous broad ruff. This appears to be covered in fine prickles but is soft to the touch. The development of the flower is prolonged, modulating gradually from a fresh green to a metallic silvery blue. By late summer, it is entirely brown and droopy but its ghost remains into the depth of winter and the structure is unmistakable. Although they are often thought of as akin to thistles, eryngiums are in fact members of the carrot family.

Height: 70cm (2¼ft) *Hardiness*: H5 *Soil*: Well-drained *Exposure*: Full sun

ERYNGIUM EBRACTEATUM

There is a sharp divide in visual characteristics between sea-hollies of the Old and New Worlds. Species from the Americas such as *E. ebracteatum* all have a forbidding basal clump of sword-shaped, serrated leaves, from the centre of which the flower spike emerges and can climb to an imposing height. Though the inflorescence bears a recognizable relation to the European sea-hollies, this can be hard to spot out of context. *E. ebracteatum* is a very airy plant, with inflorescences that superficially resemble those of a sanguisorba.
Height: 1.2m (4ft) *Hardiness*: H5
Soil: Well-drained *Exposure*: Full sun

ERYNGIUM YUCCIFOLIUM

From Central and Eastern USA, *E. yuccifolium* is one of the shorter New World species, but still reaches 1m (3¼ft) in height. It is not colourful but makes a fantastic silhouette which comes into its own later in the year.
Height: 1m (3¼ft) *Hardiness*: H4
Soil: Well-drained *Exposure*: Full sun

EUPATORIUM MACULATUM
'ATROPURPUREUM'

A robust, stately plant from the prairies of the north-eastern USA, it is late into growth but soon makes up time by flowering at a height of roughly 2m (6½ft) from midsummer onwards. The flowers are a muted rosy colour but held in broad broccoli-shaped domes, creating a distinctive silhouette which persists into the depths of winter. This plant will increase quickly for you, especially in moist rich soil.
Height: 1.5–2.5m (5–8¼ft)
Hardiness: H7 *Soil*: Not fussy, but

prefers moist, rich soil *Exposure*: Full sun or partial shade

EUPATORIUM MACULATUM 'SNOWBALL'

A strong, distinctive clone of *E. maculatum*, as the cultivar name implies it has white inflorescences that are more globular than dome-shaped. It makes a pleasing contrast in both colour and form with *Persicaria amplexicaulis* 'Orange Field' in the Oudolf Field, a combination that is repeated in the 'buttress' beds at either side of the site.
Height: 2m (6½ft) *Hardiness*: H7 *Soil*: Not fussy, but prefers moist, rich soil *Exposure*: Full sun or partial shade

EUPHORBIA GRIFFITHII 'DIXTER'

This perennial spurge from Bhutan suckers in a slightly erratic way, forming jagged-shaped networks of shoots. Their appearance in spring is dramatic, deeply suffused as they are in dark crimson. Growth is rapid, and the colour becomes slightly diluted as the shoots stretch out. When the plant flowers, however, the same intensity of colour returns to the apex. The brilliance dies down again as the plant grows more diffuse in the summer, but autumn brings more fireworks. This clone was selected by Christopher Lloyd and named for his famous garden in Sussex.
Height: 80cm (2¾ft) *Hardiness*: H7 *Soil*: Prefers moisture-retentive soil *Exposure*: Full sun or partial shade

FESTUCA MAIREI

This is a large festuca from the Atlas Mountains with fine grey foliage and slender, arching flower-stalks in summer. It occurs at altitude in its native habitat and

is therefore adapted to harsh levels of heat, drought and cold. The species is variable, with the commonest clone in cultivation being sterile. It is one of very few evergreen plants grown in the garden at Hauser & Wirth Somerset and is therefore a good 'anchor' in early spring.
Height: 1m (3¼ft) (taller in flower)
Hardiness: H7 *Soil*: Good drainage
Exposure: Full sun

FILIPENDULA RUBRA 'VENUSTA MAGNIFICA'

Called 'Queen of the Prairies' in the USA, this is like a large American version of what is known in the UK as meadowsweet. It is a stately plant, with billowing clouds of frothy, candyfloss pink flowers. The flowering performance is generous and magnificent but very short-lived, to the extent that you should probably not grow this plant, which takes up considerable space, unless you are prepared to appreciate the seedheads too. After flowering, the inflorescences fade to a dull red and thereafter to brown. It makes a valuable contribution to the winter scene.
Height: 2.5m (8¼ft) *Hardiness*: H5
Soil: Must remain moist, especially in full sun. *Exposure*: Full sun or partial shade

GENTIANA ASCLEPIADEA

'Gentian' normally brings to mind the low-growing alpine species which are all flower and barely any leaves. While the flowers on this species, known as the willow gentian, are recognizable individually as the cobalt blue trumpets typical of the genus, they are borne in the axils of long, arching herbaceous shoots in early autumn. Displayed this way they perhaps

have less impact, but the foliage structure is a bonus and the plant is easy to grow.
Height: 60cm (2ft) *Hardiness*: H5
Soil: Moist but with good drainage
Exposure: Partial shade is ideal

GERANIUM 'ROZANNE'

This deservedly popular herbaceous cranesbill arose as a hybrid of *G. himalayense* and *G. wallichianum* 'Buxton's Variety'. In the manner of the latter, it arises late from a small crown to flower freely until the first frosts, but it is bushier and more floriferous than 'Buxton's Variety'. It can be supported with twigs to give the plant a voluminous bushy habit, or equally it can be allowed to trail freely through neighbouring plants. Either way it will just keep growing and flowering in stunning profusion more than earning its keep.

Height: 50cm (20in) *Hardiness*: H7
Soil: Not fussy *Exposure*: Full sun or partial shade.

GERANIUM 'PATRICIA'

A hybrid between *G. endressii* and *G. psilostemon* with an overall impression much closer to the rather magnificent vivid magenta of the latter, but the admixture of *G. endressii* genes mellows the plant in a number of ways that are useful to gardeners. The colour is ever so slightly softer (though the dark eye of *G. psilostemon* is, crucially, retained), the height is somewhat reduced, and the flowering period is prolonged. It is a stunning plant, though like any geranium it offers nothing of interest in the winter season.

Height: 80cm (2¾ft) *Hardiness*: H7
Soil: Not fussy *Exposure*: Full sun or partial shade

LEFT
Geranium 'Spinners'
RIGHT
Gillenia trifoliata

OPPOSITE ABOVE
Gymnocladus dioica trees growing in the
apron of grass in front of the gallery
OPPOSITE BELOW LEFT
Helenium 'Loysder Wieck'
OPPOSITE BELOW RIGHT
Helenium 'Moerheim Beauty'

GERANIUM 'SPINNERS'

This pleasant blue *G. pratense* hybrid has a long season through early and midsummer, given adequate moisture. It is said to be capable of a further, late flowering if sheared to the ground in late summer. At the very least this will encourage a fresh set of leaves. There is no point in looking for winter structure from a geranium! It is used in the Wet Area of the Oudolf Field where it flowers with *Pimpinella major* 'Rosea'.
Height: 80cm (2¾ft) *Hardiness*: H7
Soil: Moist *Exposure*: Full sun

GILLENIA TRIFOLIATA

A charming and unusual plant, this bears numerous brilliant white spidery flowers, borne on dark red wiry stems that are almost invisible from a distance. Each has five irregularly disposed petals. All of this gives the plant a great feeling of animation even when it is not in motion. This is an upstanding, bushy, floriferous plant that tolerates partial shade and has a long season of interest. Furthermore, the structural form of *Gillenia trifoliata* is beautiful at all times of the year.
Height: 1m (3¼ft) *Hardiness*: H7
Soil: Not fussy *Exposure*: Full sun or partial shade

GYMNOCLADUS DIOICA

The 'Kentucky coffee tree' gained its name from the fact that Native Americans and the early settlers used to roast and grind the seeds to form the basis of a hot drink – but note that prior to roasting the seeds are highly toxic. Its winter skeleton is incredibly gaunt-looking, without any fine branches or twigs to soften its outline. The bark is roughly fissured, which contributes

to its imposing winter presence. Bi-pinnate leaves, which emerge purple in spring, transform the tree in the summer to something much less forbidding.

Height: More than 12m (39ft)
Hardiness: H5 *Soil*: Not too heavy
Exposure: Full sun

HELENIUM 'LOYSDER WIECK'

This cultivar has the tawny and marmalade colouring which is typical of the genus. The flowers are smaller and neater-looking than is typical, with a distinct gap between each petal. This gives rise to the name ('wieck' is a windmill's arm in Dutch). Late into flower, it hits its stride in August when *H.* 'Moerheim Beauty' (see below) is starting to lose its freshness. This late-season colour is harnessed in the corner beds close to the pavilion. 'Kupferzwerg' is another cultivar of *Helenium* used in the garden – it has solid red petals.

Height: 1.4m (4½ft) *Hardiness*: H7
Soil: Rich and not too well-drained
Exposure: Full sun

HELENIUM 'MOERHEIM BEAUTY'

Heleniums are perhaps the most floriferous of any daisy from the prairies. The numerous garden hybrids are derived chiefly from two species from damp meadows and streamsides: *H. autumnale* and *H. bigelovii*. In the reduced competition of border conditions, they clump up fast and will probably require splitting every other year. Given this treatment, their vigour is amazing and they will flower strongly for a long period. 'Moerheim Beauty' is a stalwart cultivar with an extraordinary rusty colouration. As long as the soil is not over-fertilized it

should not require staking.
Height: 1m (3¼ft) *Hardiness*: H7
Soil: Rich and not too well-drained
Exposure: Full sun

IMPERATA CYLINDRICA

This is a plant that Piet steered clear of for much of his career, in spite of his predilection for grasses in general. Many may still blanche at its extraordinary crimson-striped foliage. However, it is very effective in the Sporobolus Meadow, where its thick sward and colouring make it an interesting counterpoint to the sporobolus itself, as well as offering a long-lasting colour contrast to the likes of *Scabiosa columbaria* and *Allium caesium*. Intriguing in early growth, when the variegation is at its most subtle.
Height: 50cm (20in) *Hardiness*: H4
Soil: Moist but well-drained
Exposure: Full sun or partial shade

INDIGOFERA AMBLYANTHA

Among the select number of woody plants that take their place in the perennial meadow, indigofera is a shrub that flowers late on the same season's wood and can therefore be pruned hard to a framework in the spring. This fits in with the rhythm of a herbaceous planting, and the lightness of the indigofera's foliage and openness of form allow it to compete directly with the herbaceous plants that surround it rather than towering over them and creating shade.
Height: 1.5–2.5m (5–8¼ft)
Hardiness: H5 *Soil*: Well-drained
Exposure: Full sun

IRIS SIBIRICA 'PERRY'S BLUE'

This iris has an almost pan-European distribution which is much broader than its specific name suggests. Most garden forms also

borrow some genes from the Asian species *Iris sanguinea*. The flowers are individually not as spectacular as those of the bearded iris, but they are produced in great profusion over a longer period. Moreover, the plant itself is robust and trouble-free. Vigorous clumps of grassy leaves up to 1m (3¼ft) in height more than stand up for themselves at the back of a border and make a strong foliage contribution throughout the season. The seedheads also persist into the winter. 'Perry's Blue' is a pale azure cultivar, of slightly diminished size.

Height: 1m (3¼ft) *Hardiness*: H7
Soil: Rich and not too well-drained
Exposure: Full sun or partial shade

KIRENGESHOMA PALMATA

An elegant woodland native of Japan and Korea, this plant has the stature and presence to take its place in the border, although it must have shade and shelter to flourish. It is somewhat slow to get established but eventually will make a hearty clump of elegantly lobed, fat leaves, which make an admirable foil to the delicacy of the nodding pale yellow flowers. The flowers themselves are borne on dark stems, which from a distance gives them a floating quality; close-up, when the stems are more visible, the colour contrast between stem and flower adds piquancy to the effect. It is planted in the Cloister Garden, which offers the ideal conditions. Piet values it for its foliage in particular.

Height: 1m (3¼ft) *Hardiness*: H7
Soil: Moist without being too claggy *Exposure*: Requires dappled shade

KNAUTIA MACEDONICA

An extremely floriferous relative of scabious, *K. macedonica* has dark maroon pincushion flowers borne in endless profusion throughout summer. The flower stems are almost leafless and have an opposite structure, meaning that they are produced directly opposite each other on the main stem. This gives a pleasing symmetrical structure to each shoot. As a flower at the top of each shoot opens, branching occurs lower down to provide succession and this process continues indefinitely until the stem is eventually flowered to death, but others arise from the base. Old stems may be judiciously removed to encourage the production of new. It's a flimsy, short-lived sort of plant and prone to mildew, but it makes up for it by self-sowing and flowering intemperately.

Height: 75cm (2½ft) *Hardiness*: H7 *Soil*: Well-drained *Exposure*: Full sun

LIATRIS SPICATA

The pink, puffy flowers of *L. spicata* are borne on stiff spikes, which is presumably what gave rise to the specific name, though the leaves also give a bristly impression. As the plant emerges it resembles a lily more than anything else. The flowers are as fluffy and pink as you can imagine, hence the common name of 'gayfeather'.

Height: (2¾ft) *Hardiness*: H7 *Soil*: Moist but well-drained *Exposure*: Full sun

LOBELIA × SPECIOSA 'VEDRARIENSIS'

Given enough moisture, the green-leaved lobelia hybrid 'Vedrariensis' will flower plentifully throughout summer and into early

autumn. The flowers are a rich purple and with its strongly vertical intent the plant combines very well with the late-flowering umbel *Selinum wallichianum*.
Height: 1m (3¼ft) Hardiness: H5
Soil: Likes moisture Exposure: Full sun or partial shade

LYCHNIS CHALCEDONICA 'ROSEA'
Known as the 'Maltese cross', this plant is normally seen with very

bright scarlet flowers, but the form used in the garden is blush pink. It creates a strong impression with its erect, opposite growth and densely clustered terminal domes of flower.
Height: 1.2m (4ft) *Hardiness*: H7
Soil: Good drainage *Exposure*: Full sun or partial shade

LYSICHITON CAMTSCHATCENSIS
The Asian skunk cabbage is one of two members of its genus, the

other of which is native to the USA. Both are marginal aquatics which produce inflorescences early in spring, followed by clumps of coarse, handsome leaves. Being an aroid, the inflorescence is in the typical form of a spadix emerging from a spathe – as with the British native 'lords and ladies' (*Arum maculatum*), which has spawned so many bawdy folkloric names. The *Lysichiton* version of this form is

particularly gorgeous, if short-lived, but the leaves are as striking in their own way and last for most of the year.
Height: 50cm (20in) *Hardiness*: H7
Soil: Must have wet feet *Exposure*: Full sun

LYSIMACHIA EPHEMERUM
A number of loosestrife species run at the root to the extent that they cause havoc, but *L. ephemerum* is a

stately, restrained species that stays within the confines of its own clump. A notable characteristic of the plant is the dull pewter glossiness of the foliage. The small starry flowers are borne on slender spikes and are a pure white enlivened by contrast with the maroon stamens. It is not terribly long in flower, but the upright spires remain.
Height: 1.2m (4ft) *Hardiness*: H6
Soil: Likes to remain moist
Exposure: Full sun

LYTHRUM SALICARIA 'BLUSH'
A cultivar derived from the ditch-dwelling European species known as purple loosestrife, this has proved to be extremely invasive in the north-eastern USA. It is a vigorous plant and rather than the heavy purple of the species, the flowers are a much more refreshing blush pink. In contrast to 'Swirl' below, the flowers are held on definite, rather stiff spikes, and are strongly vertical.
Height: 1.2m (4ft) *Hardiness*: H6
Soil: Likes to remain moist
Exposure: Full sun

LYTHRUM VIRGATUM 'SWIRL'
Surprising though it is for a plant derived from a ditch-dwelling species, the head gardener reckons this is one of the most drought-resistant plants in the garden. This was after a thorough testing in the heatwave of 2018. It is also extremely long-flowering and appeared to remain completely unchanged after two months of punishing sunshine. The flowers are held informally, in a loose haze on wiry stems, so clouds of pink float above the Sporobolus Meadow for months in summer.

Height: 1m (3¼ft) *Hardiness*: H6
Soil: Surprisingly tolerant of
drought *Exposure*: Full sun

MOLINIA CAERULEA SUBSP. ARUNDINACEA 'TRANSPARENT'

M. caerulea is a British (and
European) native of strikingly
variable stature, such that it has
spawned a variety of garden
cultivars of different sizes and
habits. The taller varieties exhibit
more grace and movement,
sometimes at the expense of
standing well into the winter. The
common name of purple moor
grass derives from the slender
inflorescence, which is dark purple.
The distances between all the parts
of this plant are large – there is a
significant gap between the basal
clump of leaves and the point
where the flowers start to break
and the inflorescence itself is a
great deal more diffuse. This makes
for a much taller plant which is
also a great deal more see-through.
The disadvantage of this is that it
doesn't stand as well as the other
molinias – by winter's end it has
thoroughly shattered, while the
two cultivars below remain
completely unmoved.
Height: 1.8m (6ft) *Hardiness*: H7
Soil: Not fussy *Exposure*: Full sun
or partial shade

MOLINIA CAERULEA SUBSP. CAERULEA 'EDITH DUDSZUS'

As a rule, the shorter the stature,
the more rigidly structural, durable
and dense are the garden cultivars
of *M. caerulea*. 'Edith Dudzsus' is
shortish but still elegant, and
achieves a remarkably warm and
vivid autumn colouring.
Height: 70cm (2¼ft) *Hardiness*: H7
Soil: Not fussy *Exposure*: Full sun
or partial shade

LEFT
Molinia caerulea subsp. *caerulea* 'Moorhexe'
RIGHT
Monarda bradburianana seedheads

MOLINIA CAERULEA SUBSP. CAERULEA 'MOORHEXE'

'Moorhexe' is one of the lowest-growing of the purple moor grasses, more hedgehog than giraffe. It shows its adaptability both to shadier conditions and to a smaller scale through its use in the Cloister Garden. It is very different in appearance to the looser-growing molinias, somewhat resembling the spiky severity of marram grass.

The inflorescence is denser, darker and more slender than that of the more expansive varieties.
Height: 80cm (2½ft) *Hardiness*: H7 *Soil*: Not fussy *Exposure*: Full sun or partial shade

MONARDA BRADBURIANA

A bergamot which is shorter in stature than many others, this plant has a good degree of mildew resistance. Unlike many of the rangier *Monarda* cultivars based on *M. fistulosa*, it stands upright and leaves an exceptionally good winter skeleton. It bears clear soft pink flowers from mid-May, with a much earlier season than most monardas. The senescent phase also comes earlier, from mid-summer onwards but is enjoyable. It has good autumn leaf-colour.
Height: 50cm (20in) *Hardiness*: H7 *Soil*: Not fussy, but prefers not too moisture-retentive *Exposure*: Open site in full sun preferred

MYRICA GALE

A deciduous low-growing shrub which is strongly evocative of its native marshlands, the bog myrtle shows its adaptability by growing in normal border soil in the Wet Area. An interesting aspect of the planting in the Oudolf Field is that a number of different habitat

archetypes are evoked, from xerophytic grasslands to ditchside flora and wetlands, without major adjustments to soil conditions or irrigation regimes. This demonstrates how adaptable plants can be when protected from the harrowing competition of ecosystems in the wild. *Myrica gale* has glossy green leaves which look as if they should be evergreen but in fact they are not.

Height: 1.5m (5ft) *Hardiness*: H7
Soil: Likes moisture, but adaptable
Exposure: Full sun or partial shade

NEPETA GOVANIANA, N. SUBSESSILIS
These two *Nepeta* species diverge from what is generally expected of a catmint by gardeners; rather than the formless blue haze of *N.* × *faassenii*, both are plants with more subtlety and structure. *N. govaniana* has primrose-yellow flowers which are borne loosely and airily on stems just under 1m (3¼ft) tall throughout summer, while *N. subsessilis* is a much stockier plant with large blue flowers.
Height: 0.9m (3ft) *Hardiness*: H7
Soil: Unfussy *Exposure*: Full sun or partial shade

ORIGANUM LAEVIGATUM 'HOPLEYS'
A very good plant, one that not only flowers profusely over a long season (midsummer to early autumn), but also makes a useful contribution with its dark greyish-green foliage and leaves behind a fine winter skeleton. The intensely saturated colouring of the plant in flower is in large part due to the calyces, which are several tones darker than the petals. They are also more persistent and contribute their shading to the plant long after the flowers

themselves have dropped. It is combined to great effect in the garden with the fresh chartreuse of *Sesleria autumnalis*.
Height: 50cm (20in) *Hardiness*: H6 *Soil*: Good drainage required *Exposure*: Full sun

PAEONIA HYBRIDA 'DELAVAYI'

This is one of comparatively few woody species used in the Oudolf Field, all of which are planted in the beds at the perimeter of the garden. It is a characterful type of tree paeony that does not rely heavily on the beauty of its short-lived flowers. These are fairly hard to spot from a distance, but interesting close-up, glossy and dark. The shrub has a very gaunt appearance in winter and this continues until flowering time – at this point the foliage begins to emerge and take over, until presently the effect is quite luxuriantly leafy.
Height: 2.5m (8¼ft) *Hardiness*: H6 *Soil*: Not fussy *Exposure*: Full sun or partial shade

PANICUM VIRGATUM 'CLOUD NINE'

Probably the most imposing of all the varieties of grass grown in the garden, 'Cloud Nine' forms an impressive, voluminous mound of steely-grey foliage quite early in the season, erupting into blossom at a gigantic height in the late summer and autumn. It is not as colourful as 'Shenandoah' (below), but is impressive in other ways.
Height: 2.5m (8¼ft) *Hardiness*: H5 *Soil*: Not fussy, tolerant of drought *Exposure*: Full sun

PANICUM VIRGATUM 'SHENANDOAH'

In spite of its American cultivar name, this switchgrass cultivar was

discovered by the German nurseryman Hans Simon as a seedling of *P. virgatum* 'Hänse Herms'. An American species, *P. virgatum* has been developed for horticulture in European nurseries for some time and is now gaining popularity in the USA. 'Shenandoah' grows rather stealthily until it starts to become ever more noticeable in the late summer and autumn. At this point the leaf tips start colouring in russet tones, epitomizing the comforts of autumn. Compact and upright, it stands well into the winter. *Height*: 1.2m (4ft) *Hardiness*: H5 *Soil*: Not fussy, tolerant of drought *Exposure*: Full sun

PAPAVER ORIENTALE 'KARINE' AND 'SCARLETT O'HARA'

Oriental poppies are the most substantial plants among herbaceous poppies, discounting the genus *Macleaya*. Their season of growth is opposite to that of prairie perennials – it starts in autumn and the plants will often remain green throughout the British winter unless it is a harsh one. Vegetative growth builds up to a flowering in late spring, after which the plants go dormant. The flowering is fairly short – three weeks at most – but so eye-catching that they are well worth growing to provide flower power at a stage when many prairie plants are lacking interest. The complementary growth season helps, as there is little direct competition for light with the main crop of later-flowering perennials. 'Karine' is a soft salmon pink; the cultivar name 'Scarlett O'Hara' speaks for itself. To date the oriental poppies have struggled to establish

themselves in the garden, perhaps due to drainage issues.
Height: 80cm (2¾ft) *Hardiness*: H7 *Soil*: Good drainage *Exposure*: Open site in full sun preferred

PENNISETUM ALOPECUROIDES F. VIRIDESCENS

This is a fantastic, tactile grass that comes into flower late in the season. The flowerheads are of a fascinating shimmery purple smoke and are quite translucent. Not hardy in continental climates, but grows well in Somerset (where the temperature rarely drops below -10C/14F) given good drainage.
Height: 80cm (2¾ft) *Hardiness*: H3 *Soil*: Needs good drainage *Exposure*: Full sun

PENSTEMON DIGITALIS 'HUSKER'S RED'

P. digitalis is rather atypical of the genus as commonly known to gardeners in a number of ways. It is earlier in flower (late spring), somewhat shade-tolerant and truly herbaceous, as opposed to those sub-shrubby penstemons that become quite woody at the base. Altogether it is a subtler performer, with some delicacy in the disposition of its flowers. The space between them allows them to nod elegantly. 'Husker's Red' is named for the colour of the young foliage, which animates the spring scene and contrasts well with the white flowers.
Height: 60cm (2ft) *Hardiness*: H5 *Soil*: Good drainage *Exposure*: Full sun or partial shade

PEROVSKIA ATRIPLICIFOLIA

This plant is known as 'Russian sage', although it is actually a native of the Himalayas and western China. It is a commonly grown

sub-shrub which although inclined to flop stays pleasingly upright in the Oudolf Field, due to good exposure and lack of excessive fertilization. *Perovskia atriplicifolia* makes a great contrast in colour and form with *Sedum* 'Matrona' and shares its long, late flowering season.
Height: 1.2m (4ft) *Hardiness*: H5
Soil: Good drainage *Exposure*: Open site in full sun

PERSICARIA AMPLEXICAULIS 'ALBA', 'FIREDANCE' AND 'ORANGE FIELD'

P. amplexicaulis offers one of the most vigorous and long-lasting flowering displays of any herbaceous plant. Critics may point to the coarseness of its leaves, akin to those of a dock, which is in the same family – but if you are in the business of creating naturalistic planting schemes it should not trouble you too much when plants resemble weeds. 'Firedance' is a strong brickish-red. With 'Alba', the leavening effect on this species of having white flowers is quite marked by contrast with the strong colours of other cultivars. Where we normally see an unashamedly assertive plant that bristles with strong colour and coarse growth, the attenuated inflorescence of 'Alba' is translucent and ethereal. 'Orange Field' is stockier and bushier with shorter inflorescences held closer to a dense mound of foliage. The colour is an extraordinarily luminous coral-pink.
Height: 1m (3 ¼ ft) *Hardiness*: H7
Soil: Appreciates retentive soil, but not fussy *Exposure*: Full sun or partial shade

PHLOMIS RUSSELIANA

From a creeping, matted, rhizomatous rootstock this herbaceous

Phlomis produces felty leaves and tall stems with flowers in distinctly tiered circles. However, the plant is really all about the architecture of its seedheads, which are already brown and solidified by midsummer but persist heartily until they are removed the following year. This plant increases quite quickly in all directions and may need to be controlled by splitting every other year or so.

Height: 1m (3¼ft) *Hardiness*: H6
Soil: Not fussy *Exposure*: Full sun

PIMPINELLA MAJOR 'ROSEA'
In the Oudolf Field, this follows in the succession of pretty pink umbels shortly after *Chaerophyllum hirsutum* 'Roseum'. Its foliage is sparser, which highlights its structural qualities. It flowers in the Wet Area along with *Campanula* 'Sarastro', *Geranium* 'Spinners' and

Lythrum salicaria 'Blush'.
Height: 1m (3¼ft) *Hardiness*: H7
Soil: Not fussy *Exposure*: Full sun

PONTEDERIA CORDATA
An endearing plant for pond margins, *P. cordata* produces spikes of rich blue flowers in midsummer. It needs to be planted at a decent depth with 5–15cm (2–6in) water above it so that the crown is not exposed to freezing in the winter.

Height: 1m (3¼ft) *Hardiness*: H5
Soil: Marginal aquatic *Exposure*: Full sun or partial shade

PYCNANTHEMUM MUTICUM
This plant is a favourite of Piet's and he used it to great effect on the High Line in New York, but it is at best a rather sporadic grower in this Somerset garden to date. The reason for this is not entirely clear, but it may be related to the

soil compaction problems in some of the beds.

Height: 1m (3¼ft) *Hardiness*: H7 *Soil*: Said to be unfussy, but this may be the issue in the garden, where the soil is heavy and in places compacted. *Exposure*: Full sun or partial shade

RUDBECKIA SUBTOMENTOSA
A plant which is perhaps best known in the guise of the cultivar 'Henry Eilers', which has rolled-up petals. The species in general is variable in a number of key characteristics such as the size of the flowers and how bright yellow they are. This can alter the overall effect of the plant quite consider-ably from one of subtlety to a rather glary slab of yellow.

Height: 1.5m (5ft) *Hardiness*: H6 *Soil*: Normal garden soil, not too dry *Exposure*: Full sun

RUELLIA HUMILIS
Known as 'wild petunia' in the USA, this member of the Acan-thaceae family is nothing of the sort. Piet likes to use it in prairie-type schemes to help cover areas of bare soil. It is a low-growing herb with pale-lilac flowers and soft, pubescent leaves. In the Lurie Gardens in Chicago it has become something of a pest and has to be kept in check. There are no such

problems in Somerset, where it seems to struggle to gain a foothold in the Sporobolus Meadow.

Height: 30cm (12in) *Hardiness*: H7 *Soil*: Not too wet, tolerant of drought *Exposure*: Full sun

SALVIA X SYLVESTRIS 'DEAR ANJA'
The long, upstanding flower-spikes of this salvia make a considerable impression in early and midsum-

mer, when the richness of their colouring and strong structure draw the eye. It is lovely in combination with *Achillea* 'Credo' and *Geranium* 'Patricia'. The spikes and calyces persist after the flowers have dropped. Many *Salvia* × *sylvestris* cultivars will reflower on shorter spikes if dead-headed, but that would make the upright structure of the plant less emphatic as it drifts into senescence.

Height: 90cm (3ft) *Hardiness*: H7 *Soil*: Good drainage *Exposure*: Open site in full sun

SALVIA VERTICILLATA 'PURPLE RAIN'

This is not much of a plant to provide structure, nor winter interest. Its tissues are soft and floppy and it sprawls indefinitely. In that sense it is an atypical 'Oudolf plant', but it earns its keep by flowering incontinently and the flower-heads themselves do have some architectural sensibility, in that the flowers are displayed in strongly distinct whorls from the base of the stem upwards. As with many salvias, the colourful calyces make an important contribution to the overall effect, and they persist considerably longer than the flowers themselves.

Height: 50cm (1½ft) *Hardiness*: H5 *Soil*: Not fussy *Exposure*: Full sun

SANGUISORBA CANADENSIS, S. OFFICINALIS 'BLACKTHORN', 'BURY COURT' AND 'RED BUTTONS'

The genus *Sanguisorba* has become immensely popular of late, and Piet has done a considerable amount to promote these lovely plants. Members of the genus vary considerably in stature, but as a group they are characterized by an airy grace and very compact flowerheads. 'Red Buttons' has

intensely saturated dark red inflorescences which are small and almost perfectly globular; 'Bury Court' is quite similar but even more magnificent in stature, with flowerheads that are slightly elongated in comparison to 'Red Buttons'. 'Blackthorn' has a much laxer, longer inflorescence which is soft pink, while the flowerheads of *S. canadensis* are made up of silky white tassles.

SANGUISORBA CANADENSIS: *Height*: 1.6m (5¼ft) *Hardiness*: H7 *Soil*: Moist but with decent drainage *Exposure*: Full sun or partial shade
SANGUISORBA 'BLACKTHORN': *Height*: 1.8m (6ft) *Hardiness*: H7 *Soil*: Moist but with decent drainage *Exposure*: Full sun or partial shade
SANGUISORBA 'BURY COURT': *Height*: 2m (6½ft) *Hardiness*: H7 *Soil*: Moist but with decent drainage *Exposure*: Full sun or partial shade

SANGUISORBA 'RED BUTTONS': *Height*: 0.9m (3ft) *Hardiness*: H7 *Soil*: Moist but with decent drainage *Exposure*: Full sun or partial shade

SCUTELLARIA INCANA

An adaptable and tough plant, *S. incana* brings a real injection of freshness to flowerbeds throughout the latter half of summer. The numerous flowers, borne in a

candelabra formation, are a chalky blue, which contrasts to great effect with the growing accretion of dun-like colours as autumn approaches.
Height: 1m (3¼ft) *Hardiness*: H7 *Soil*: Not fussy *Exposure*: Full sun or partial shade

SCABIOSA COLUMBARIA

This chalky blue South African scabious species is also known in

its pale lemon-yellow form, subsp.
ochroleuca. It is a flimsy, ephemeral
plant, but one which flowers
continuously over a long period
in the summer. While it is not
long-lived, it is a great self-sower,
so it relies on the open conditions
among the sporobolus and the
forbearance of the gardeners for it
to persist. It is an integral part of
the Sporobolus Meadow, that
diaphanous tapestry at the heart

of the Oudolf Field.
Height: 0.9m (3ft) *Hardiness*: H4
Soil: Well-drained *Exposure*: Full sun

SEDUM 'MATRONA'
(NOW HYLOTELEPHIUM 'MATRONA')

'Matrona' is perhaps the best sedum
in terms of its foliage contribution.
From early in the year the leaves
are large and of an interesting
pewter colour, suffused with
magical pinkish tones. Although

short in stature, it has the presence
to act as an anchor point and grows
neatly enough to be placed at the
front of the border.
Height: 0.6m (2ft) *Hardiness*: H7
Soil: Well-drained *Exposure*: Full sun

SELINUM WALLICHIANUM

This is a late-flowering umbellifer,
which is a rare and welcome thing,
and the lustrous foliage makes a
sterling contribution right up to

and including the time of
flowering in mid to late summer.
It has been described by Piet as
'troublesome and capricious' and
perhaps has a tendency to disappear
when undernourished. However in
rich soil of a decent depth it is a
reliable plant.
Height: 1.5m (5ft) *Hardiness*: H6
Soil: Requires fertile soil to a good
depth *Exposure*: Open site in full
sun preferred

SERRATULA TINCTORIA VAR. SEOANEI

A herbaceous border plant in miniature, this has considerable charm. It is a rigidly structured, upstanding knapweed that is quite as recognizable in winter as at any other time of year. It flowers over a long period from summer to autumn, with miniature knapweed-type flowers in great profusion. Neat, stocky and with appealing wiry foliage, it is used most extensively in the Wet Area of the Oudolf Field.
Height: 40cm (16in) *Hardiness*: H6
Soil: Not fussy *Exposure*: Full sun or partial shade

SESLERIA AUTUMNALIS

This is a neat, clump-forming grass which makes a very solid 'buttress' plant. Its leaves are a particularly constant chartreuse green and the plant is quite eye-catching in its subtle way, but a special strength is that in combination with other plants it will enhance the vibrancy of other colours. In the Oudolf Field, a substantial grouping of this plant is often the first thing that catches the eye as you survey the garden from the direction of the gallery. Its sward remains clumpy and dense throughout winter and if anything the slender inflorescences stand out more during this season.

Piet has also planted this adaptable and dependable species in the slightly shady Cloister Garden at the gallery.
Height: 50cm (1½ft) *Hardiness*: H7
Soil: Prefers good drainage
Exposure: Full sun or partial shade

SESLERIA 'GREENLEE'

A more compact and much darker-leaved grass than *S. autumnalis*, 'Greenlee' was drafted in to replace

Briza media 'Limouzi' (which struggled to establish in the hotter than expected Somerset sun) as the matrix grass in the Wet Area of the Oudolf Field. *Sesleria* 'Greenlee' has proved to be a good choice in that it is a suitably resilient plant and does a good job of evoking wetlands.
Height: 50cm (20in) *Hardiness*: H7
Soil: Very adaptable *Exposure*: Full sun or partial shade

SPODIOPOGON SIBIRICUS
A tall grass which is late to emerge in the spring and starts rather weakly, *S. sibiricus* makes up for lost time once temperatures are warmer and becomes quite a dominant feature of the landscape. It is one of the chief components of the planting in the Magnolia Bed in the farmyard, and is also used on the fringes of the Oudolf Field. The panicles shimmer markedly when backlit by the sun and the plant has good autumn colour. It colonizes a bit at the root and then likes to form quite dense, tall clumps.
Height: 1.6m (5¼ft) *Hardiness*: H7
Soil: Moist but well-drained
Exposure: Full sun or partial shade

SPOROBOLUS HETEROLEPIS
This is one of the few genuine prairie grasses that adapts well to conditions in the UK. Its numerous leaves are so fine, especially when desiccated and laid low by the winter, as to give the impression of brush strokes. When planted en masse its inflorescence, whether in flower or seed, creates a gauzy haze at the height of about 0.8–1m (2¾–3¼ft). The ultimate matrix plant, it exists to bring the best out of other plants around it rather than draw attention to itself. In

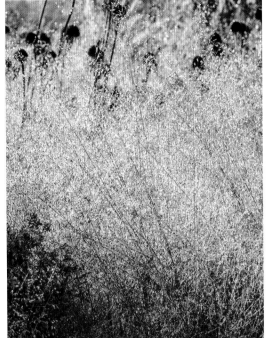

winter the dense solidity of echinacea cones and phlomis seed-heads stand out against it in strong relief. It is scented of coriander and popcorn
Height: 60cm (2ft) in leaf, 90cm (3ft) in flower *Hardiness*: H7 *Soil*: Well-drained *Exposure*: Full sun

STACHYS OFFICINALIS 'HUMMELO'
An archetypal Oudolf plant, *S. officinalis* 'Hummelo' is named for his garden in the Netherlands. It is a high-performing clone of the European native betony, with densely packed flower spikes, good colouring and a long season from summer to early autumn. It is as neat and structured in senescence and death as it is in full flower.
Height: 70cm (2¼ft) *Hardiness*: H7 *Soil*: Prefers good drainage *Exposure*: Position in full sun or partial shade

STACHYS OFFICINALIS 'ROSEA'
Similar to the *Stachys officinalis* 'Hummelo', but a much softer pink, and slightly laxer in the production of its flowers. This is not necessarily a bad thing – if anything it has slightly more natural grace than 'Hummelo'.
Height: 70cm (2¼ft) *Hardiness*: H7 *Soil*: Prefers good drainage *Exposure*: Position in full sun or partial shade

STIPA TENUISSIMA
At all times of year this stipa offers the softest, most yielding clump of living and dead foliage, but in early summer it erupts into a particular enhanced glossy featheriness as it flowers. It is one of the very few evergreens in the planting of the Oudolf Field and is thus of value in early spring, when foliage is in short supply.
Height: 70cm (2¼ft) *Hardiness*: H4

Soil: Good drainage required
Exposure: Full sun

SUCCISA PRATENSIS

The 'devil's bit scabious' is supported by a basal clump of broad, smooth leaves. The tall flowering stems are practically leafless, so that the pincushion heads of flowers appear to float. On closer inspection they are supported by wiry stems of opposite growth. It is an airy plant, the effect of which owes as much to the space between the flowers as to the flowers themselves. The colour is a very unusual, smoky purple. It has the strength to mix it with the rambunctious flora of ditches but retains a pleasing grace. *Height*: 1m (3¼ft) *Hardiness*: H7 *Soil*: Likes to stay wet all year. Good on clay. *Exposure*: Full sun or partial shade

THALICTRUM DELAVAYI

The most graceful of meadow rues, with flowers and foliage as delicate as any choice woodlander or alpine, but the plant is tall and robust enough to hold its own in a busy border. Nevertheless, it is so unobtrusive in the early months of the year that its presence could easily be forgotten until you notice it flowering in midsummer. In the Oudolf Field, Piet uses it in a repeating combination with the willow gentian (*Gentiana asclepia-dea*). Its airiness allows room for more stocky solid plants around it. *T. rochebruneanum* is similar and the two often seem to get mixed up in the trade, but *T. rochebruneanum* is said to be considerably taller. *Height*: 1.2m (4ft) *Hardiness*: H7 *Soil*: Adaptable, but prefers to stay moist. *Exposure*: Full sun or partial shade

THALICTRUM 'ELIN'

One of the most determinedly tall and upright thalictrums, 'Elin' doesn't have the grace of *T. delavayi* but makes up for that in sheer presence, height and strength. The leaves, when they appear in spring, have the colour of purple sprouting broccoli. Growth from early spring is rampant, especially when compared to the timid, late first appearance of *T. delavayi* and other similar types. It derives its hybrid vigour from a cross between *T. flavum* subsp. *glaucum* and *T. rochebruneanum*. The pale lilac flowers are borne in midsummer.
Height: 2.5m (8¼ft) *Hardiness*: H7
Soil: Moist, rich and fertile
Exposure: Full sun if it is not to flop

TRICYRTIS FORMOSANA

Spectacular in close-up, elegant in the middle distance but almost invisible from far away, *T. formosana* repays close inspection, the intricacy of its flowers matched by the elegance of their disposition atop stems with pleasingly curved and pleated leaves. One of the joys of Piet's planting is that as well as creating a cogent whole, his designs encourage contemplation of plants and their form as individuals.
Height: 50–70cm (1¾–2¼ft)
Hardiness: H5 *Soil*: Moist but well-drained soil required
Exposure: Sun or shade

VERONICASTRUM 'ADORATION', 'DIANE' AND 'ERICA'

Derived from a prairie species with a wide distribution along the east coast of the USA, veronicastrums are best known for their flowers, which are pink, lilac or white. These are displayed on elegant, slender, tall spikes and soon fade,

BELOW LEFT
Veronicastrum 'Diane'
BELOW RIGHT
Vitex agnus-castus 'Silver Spire'

OPPOSITE
Nectaroscordum tripedale

but the magnificence of the structure remains. Before the plant flowers, the foliage makes a very strong impression in contrast with the fresh shoots of other plants, as it is dark bronzy-green and held in whorls which create significant shadowy voids beneath them. The flowers of 'Adoration' are a pale, smoky lilac-pink – it seems to be the earliest into growth and has shorter but more numerous

branched spikes. 'Erica' has an even paler pink flower, and long, slender flower spikes. The more concentrated colour of the buds at the top of the flower-spike makes a telling contribution in contrast with the unopened flowers. 'Diane' contributes a lovely ethereal effect with its white flowers.
Height: 1.5m (5ft) *Hardiness*: H7
Soil: Adaptable, but prefers to stay moist. *Exposure*: Full sun

VITEX AGNUS-CASTUS 'SILVER SPIRE'
This is one of the very few woody species planted in the Oudolf Field. However, due to its pruning regime which requires it to be cut back to a low framework of branches in early spring, its growth habit and maintenance are really rather similar to that of a herbaceous plant. The leaves are reminiscent of the cannabis plant but are much smoother and

without the jagged edge. The scented flowers are borne on spikes during mid and late summer. It is not frequently seen in the UK, perhaps due to its lack of hardiness, but it has survived relatively harsh winters in Somerset. It takes its place on the wild fringes of the Oudolf Field.
Height: up to 2m (6½ft) Hardiness: H4 Soil: Good drainage required Exposure: Full sun

ALLIUM ATROPURPUREUM

A striking component of the early summer scene in the Oudolf Field, *A. atropurpureum* has hemispherical flowerheads of the darkest maroon held tall enough to hoist them above clumps of heleniums. It makes a great contrast with *Salvia × sylvestris* 'Dear Anja' and even more so the pale blue flowers of *Amsonia hubrichtii*.
Height: 80cm (2¾ft) *Hardiness*: H5

Soil: Good drainage *Exposure*: Open site in full sun

ALLIUM CAESIUM

This is a long-flowering, chalky-blue allium with a flower-head similar to the better-known *A. caeruleum* but lower to the ground. *A. caesium* enlivens the sward of the Sporobolus Meadow in early summer, making a lovely contrast with the red-leaved grass *Imperata* *cylindrica* and coinciding with the first flowers of *Dianthus carthusianorum*. Not commonly cultivated, it appears to thrive in the open conditions of the Oudolf Field.
Height: 30cm (12in) *Hardiness*: H7
Soil: Good drainage *Exposure*: Open site in full sun

ALLIUM CHRISTOPHII

This is commonly planted and among the most spectacular ornamental onions, although the flowers are almost colourless when they open and sit quite low to the ground. The inflorescence can be compared to a cluster of fireworks at the point of explosion. It dries well and in this state its intriguing flower structure can last the summer.
Height: 50cm (20in) *Hardiness*: H5
Soil: Prefers good drainage but not fussy *Exposure*: Full sun

OPPOSITE
Allium atropurpureum in flower (left)
and seed (right)

BELOW, LEFT
Camassia leichtlinii
BELOW, RIGHT
Dodecatheon jeffreyi

ANEMONE NEMOROSA 'LISMORE BLUE'

'Lismore Blue' is a form of the European native woodland anemone with large, pale blue flowers that Piet grows in his own garden, Hummelo. It can be grown in association with herbaceous plants, which only exclude light from the anemones as they begin to go over. It is planted in the Wet Area of the Oudolf Field.
Height: 10cm (4in) *Hardiness*: H7

Soil: Likes moisture *Exposure*: Full sun or partial shade while in growth.

CAMASSIA LEICHTLINII

Prairie plantings naturally tend to go through a comparatively flat, featureless period in spring, because most perennials and grasses are deciduous and fairly late to get moving. However, nature abhors a vacuum, and bulbs are well equipped to take advantage of this lull in competition for light and moisture. By storing energy from the previous year's growth, they are able to burst into life and exploit all the gaps. There are comparatively few spring bulbs that grow to a decent height, and this makes *Camassia leichtlinii* valuable for late spring borders. An imposing spike of blue flowers arises from a clump of strappy leaves.

Height: 80cm (2¾ft) *Hardiness*: H4
Soil: Enjoys moisture *Exposure*: Full sun or light shade

DODECATHEON JEFFREYI

Although not technically a bulbous genus, *Dodecatheon* (of the primrose family) is sometimes included in bulb lists because it undergoes a summer dormancy (or aestivation) in common with most spring flowering bulbs. It also possesses

ABOVE
Eremurus 'Romance'

BELOW LEFT AND RIGHT
Fritillaria meleagris

the delicacy and cheerfulness that we associate with woodland bulbous flora. Because it requires no light in summer it can be situated among clumps of perennials that will smother it when they are in full growth. It is used in the Cloister Garden, where it emerges among patches of *Sesleria autumnalis*.
Height: 30cm (12in) *Hardiness*: H7 *Soil*: Moist in the spring, will

tolerate summer drought *Exposure*: Deciduous shade

EREMURUS 'ROMANCE'
Eremurus are remarkably imposing and graceful in flower, but generally considered very difficult to keep. One reason for this is that the fleshy roots spread over a long distance horizontally from the crown of the plant, and they deeply resent disturbance. In addition, they

dislike competition above ground when in growth. Piet's planting style caters for these requirements, as he prefers to create fairly stable plant communities with long-lived perennials, so there is generally rather less digging and disturbance than is traditional in an 'English' garden. Also, conditions are generally quite open in spring, with prairie perennials generally quite late into growth and without

the pervasive smothering influence of forget-me-nots.
Height: 1.2-1.5m (4–5ft) *Hardiness*: H7 *Soil*: Must have good drainage. *Exposure*: Full sun must reach its basal leaves in growth

FRITILLARIA MELEAGRIS
The snake's head fritillary is an extraordinary, moody occupant of European damp meadows; I have even seen it flowering while

submerged in water one wet spring in Oxford. Therefore, it makes a suitable addition to the Wet Area planting adjacent to the pond. The nodding flowers have an eye-catching mottled chequerboard pattern on their petals.
Height: 30cm (12in) *Hardiness*: H5
Soil: Likes to stay moist but is somewhat adaptable *Exposure*: Prefers full sun in growth, but deciduous shade is acceptable

LEUCOJUM AESTIVUM

The so-called summer snowflake actually flowers quite early in the spring. It is an imposing plant with a juicy clump of leaves and nodding flowers held aloft on tall scapes. The spring snowflake flowers even earlier, in February.
Height: 50cm (20in) *Hardiness*: H7
Soil: Likes moisture but is adaptable *Exposure*: Full sun in growth, but deciduous shade is acceptable

LILIUM MARTAGON

A European lily that emerges in spring to flower in early summer, its strong form even prior to flowering is well displayed in the Cloister Garden, where it arises from clumps of *Sesleria autumnalis* with *Euphorbia griffithii* 'Dixter' beneath the paper mulberry trees. It is known as the turkscap lily, which is descriptive of the severely reflexed, downward-pointing flowers. Like all lilies it is vulnerable to lily beetle larvae, which must be controlled by picking off or spraying.
Height: 75cm (2½ft) *Hardiness*: H7
Soil: Well-drained *Exposure*: Full sun or ideally light shade

MUSCARI ARMENIACUM 'VALERIE FINNIS'

While this is a diminutive bulb it has plenty of impact nonetheless due to the eye-catching colour of

its flowers, which are a very pale blue. It is delicate in appearance but robust in growth.
Height: 20cm (8in) *Hardiness*: H6 *Soil*: Well-drained *Exposure*: Full sun or partial, deciduous shade.

NECTAROSCORDUM SICULUM
Pale and interesting cousins of *Allium*, *Nectaroscordum* flowers are pendent and borne at the top of tall, smooth stems. The pink, green and cream colouring is generally somewhat mottled and muted when your view is of the exterior of the petals, and as the flowers hang down that will generally be the case unless you make a special effort to get down low enough to look up into the flower.
Height: 1–1.5m (3¼–5ft) *Hardiness*: H5 *Soil*: Well-drained *Exposure*: Position this plant in full sun or part shade.

NECTAROSCORDUM TRIPEDALE
As it doesn't produce offsets and takes six years from seed, *Nectaroscordum tripedale* fits rather well in the rarefied atmosphere of the Cloister Garden, which in general has a somewhat otherworldly feeling. Considered one of the best ornamental onions of all, it shares the subtle grace of other *Nectaroscordum* species, but is prettier, with clear pale pink and white flowers.
Height: 1m (3¼ft) *Hardiness*: H5 *Soil*: Well-drained *Exposure*: Full sun or part shade.

SCILLA PERUVIANA
This scilla, although not very tall, has a good deal of presence due to its broad, conical, intense blue inflorescence in mid to late spring. In the Cloister Garden, it flowers concurrently with *Nectaroscordum tripedale*. It is a Mediterranean bulb

with a misleading name derived from the fact that it was originally transported to the UK on a ship named The Peru.
Height: 40cm (16in) *Hardiness*: H4
Soil: Well-drained *Exposure*: Full sun

TRILLIUM SESSILE

Trilliums are reputed to be difficult, being equally likely to succumb to poor drainage in winter or drought in the summer. They are also very vulnerable to predation by slugs and snails. Nevertheless, this species is growing in the Oudolf Field, planted in association with *Astilboides tabularis*. Piet is generally not one to pursue 'choice' plants that are achingly hard to grow and interestingly this particular trillium appears to hold its own in the Wet Area without any special treatment. It is a subtle presence in April with its nodding, wine-red flowers.

Height: 20cm (8in) *Hardiness*: H7
Soil: Moist but well-drained
Exposure: Deciduous shade

Glossary

Aestivation As opposed to hibernation, aestivation is a seasonal dormancy which takes place in the summer rather than the winter. Most spring-flowering bulbs and a number of early herbaceous perennials undergo aestivation.

Basal Derived from the base of the plant, for example basal leaves which appear to grow directly from the ground rather than from an aerial stem.

Calyx (pl. calyces) The collective term for the sepals of a flower. Sepals protect the petals in bud and support it when in flower. They are often green and not very noticeable, but occasionally (notably in the genus *Salvia*) they add their own colour to that of the petals.

Clone Many garden plants must be propagated asexually in order to retain the same characteristics that distinguish them. Taking cuttings, splitting herbaceous plants and micropropagation are all techniques which duplicate plants with exactly the same genetic make-up.

Compound leaf A leaf composed of several parts or leaflets, for example, those of ash and horse chestnut trees.

Corolla Collective term for the petals of a flower.

Cruciform In the shape of a cross, for example any flower belonging to the cabbage (Brassicaceae) family.

Cultivar Short for 'cultivated variety'. A distinctive form of a plant with garden-worthy characteristics. Very often these characteristics are preserved by clonal propagation, but if the desired characteristics remain stable from seed-grown plants, they may also be produced by sexual means.

Herbaceous Plants that produce no permanent or woody structure above ground, as opposed to trees or shrubs.

Heteroblasty Some plants produce different leaf types at different stages of their growth. A well-known example is that of *Eucalyptus*, the juvenile leaves of which are popular with florists. At Hauser & Wirth Somerset, the *Broussonetia* trees in the cloister exhibit this characteristic.

Inflorescence The unit of a group of flowers held together in one structure, or the disposition of flowers on a plant. A daisy head, for instance, which is popularly thought of as a flower, is correctly termed an inflorescence as it is composed of multiple tiny flowers.

Mesophytic Describes a plant that thrives in intermediate conditions with regard to the levels of sunlight and moisture.

Perennial Technically, any plant that persists for an indefinite period beyond a couple of years, including woody and bulbous flora. In general, it is understood to mean non-bulbous herbaceous perennials.

Ray florets A daisy inflorescence composed of numerous small flowers (called 'florets'), of two types. The tiny 'disc' florets form the centre of the structure, with the more conspicuous 'rays' radiating outwards.

Scape A flower stem that arises directly from the rootstock of a plant.

Senescent Tissue that is ageing rather than growing actively.

Spathe In the arum family (Araceae), typically the flowering structure is partially enclosed by a broad spathe (a type of bract), often to great ornamental effect.

Stamens The male, pollen-bearing part of a flower. Occasionally these can be quite showy, as in with the flowers of *Amorpha canescens*.

Suckers A shoot which arises directly from the root of the plant, generally at some distance away from the main structure of a shrub.

Umbel The typical form of the inflorescence in the carrot family. Flower stalks of a similar length spring from a common point and form a domed or flat surface, which is circular when viewed from above.

Xerophytic Refers to plants that live in a dry habitat that can tolerate low water levels and periods of drought.

Further reading

Piet Oudolf

Oudolf, Piet, and Noel Kingsbury. *Planting: A New Perspective*. Timber Press, Portland and London, 2013.

Oudolf, Piet, and Noel Kingsbury. *Hummelo*. Monacelli Press, New York, 2015.

Oudolf, Piet, and Henk Gerritsen. *Dream Plants for the Natural Garden*. Frances Lincoln, London, 2013.

Oudolf, Piet, and Rick Darke. *Gardens of the High Line*. Timber Press, Portland, 2017.

The New Perennial Movement

Dunnett, Nigel, and James Hitchmough. *The Dynamic Landscape: Design, Ecology and Management of Naturalistic Urban Planting*. Spon Press, Abingdon, 2004.

Hansen, Richard, and Friedrich Strahl. *Perennials and their Garden Habitats*. Cambridge University Press, Cambridge, 1993.

Kingsbury, Noel. *The New Perennial Garden*. Frances Lincoln, London, 1996.

William Robinson and the English naturalistic style

Chatto, Beth. *Beth Chatto's Damp Garden: Moisture-Loving Plants for Year-Round Interest*. Cassell, London, 2005.

Chatto, Beth. *Beth Chatto's Gravel Garden*. Frances Lincoln, London, 2000.

Lloyd, Christopher. *Succession Planting for Adventurous Gardeners*. BBC Books, London, 2005.

Lloyd, Christopher, and Fergus Garrett. *Meadows at Great Dixter and Beyond*. Pimpernel Press, London, 2016.

Robinson, William. *The English Flower Garden*. John Murray, London, 1883.

Robinson, William. *The Wild Garden*. John Murray, London, 1870.

Hauser & Wirth Somerset

Burkhalter, Gabriela, and Alice Workman (editors). *Beyond the Town: Conversations of Art and Land*. Hauser & Wirth Publishers, 2018.

Plant nurseries

UK

Trade Nurseries

Arvensis Perennials
Lower Wraxall
Bradford-on-Avon
Wiltshire
BA15 2RU
www.arvensisperennials.co.uk

Orchard Dene Nurseries
Lower Assendon
Henley on Thames
Oxon RG9 6AL
www.orcharddene.co.uk

Nurseries open to the general public

Avondale Nursery, at Russell's Nursery
Mill Hill
Baginton
Coventry
CV8 3AG
www.avondalenursery.co.uk

Ballyrobert Gardens
154 Ballyrobert Road
Ballyclare
Co. Antrim
BT39 9RT
www.ballyrobertgardens.com

Beth Chatto Nurseries
Elmstead Market
Clacton Road
Elmstead
Colchester
Essex
CO7 7DB
www.bethchatto.co.uk

Cotswold Garden Flowers
Sands Lane
Badsey
Evesham
Worcestershire
WR11 7EZ
www.cgf.net

Dove Cottage Nursery & Garden
Shibden Hall Road
Halifax HX3 9XA
West Yorkshire
www.dovecottagenursery.co.uk

Hardy's Cottage Garden Plants
Priory Lane Nursery
Freefolk Priors
Whitchurch
Hampshire
RG28 7FA
www.hardysplants.co.uk

Knoll Gardens
Stapehill Road
Hampreston
Wimborne BH21 7ND
www.knollgardens.co.uk

Marchants Hardy Plants
2 Marchants Cottages
Mill Lane
Laughton
E. Sussex
BN8 6AJ
www.marchantshardyplants.co.uk

The Plant Specialist
Whitefield Lane
Great Missenden
Buckinghamshire
HP16 0BH
www.theplantspecialist.co.uk

Austria
Sarastro-Stauden
Ort 131
4974 Ort im Innkreis
www.sarastro-stauden.com

France
Les Vivaces de Sandrine et Thierry
40 Rue Roger Salengro
59496, Hantay
www.les-vivaces-de-sandrine-et-thierry.fr

Germany
Anja Maubach
Arends Staudengärtnerei –
Gartenschule – Gartenplanung
Monschaustraße 76
42 369 Wuppertal
www.arends-maubach.de

Staudengärtnerei Gaißmayer GmbH & Co.
KG
Jungviehweide 3
89257 Illertissen
www.gaissmayer.de

Die Staudengärtnerei Till Hofmann und
Fine Molz GbR
Alte Iphöfer Straße 27
97348 Rödelsee
www.die-staudengaertnerei.de

The Netherlands
De Hessenhof
Hessenweg 41
6718 TC Ede
www.hessenhof.nl

Kwekerij De Kleine Plantage
Handerweg 1 – 9967 TC Eenrum
www.dekleineplantage.nl

Kwekerij In Goede Aarde
Kapitalendam 7
4522PT-Biervliet
www.kwekerij-ingoedeaarde.nl

Index

Page numbers in *italic* type refer to pictures or their captions.

About the author

Rory Dusoir decided to pursue a career in horticulture while studying for a classics degree at Balliol College, Oxford. After graduating, he worked at Great Dixter as assistant head gardener prior to undertaking the prestigious Kew Diploma. While studying at the Royal Botanic Gardens, Kew he won a travel scholarship to study the Hungarian grasslands, an eye-opening visit which affirmed his interest in wild plant communities. He has been head gardener at Howe Mill, on the bank of the River Kennet in Wiltshire and most recently at Stud House, a private estate within the grounds of Hampton Court Palace. During these years, he was given some freedom to develop his own distinctive planting style. Rory has written on a wide range of horticultural topics for the *Daily Telegraph*, *RHS Garden* magazine and *Gardens Illustrated*, and has also contributed to two books: *Plant User Handbook* and *Roses: A Celebration*. In 2016, Rory set up a garden installation, consultancy and maintenance company 'Kennedy Song Dusoir' with two fellow students of the Kew Diploma, Jeeun Song-Dusoir and Phil Kennedy. Based in London, they focus on creative design, installation and maintenance of landscapes and gardens.

Acknowledgements

I owe a huge debt of gratitude to my editor, Anna Mumford, who has been nothing but patient in guiding me through the production of this, my first book. I am also indebted to our photographer Jason, who made a massive crepuscular effort to capture the magic of the garden in many different moods. Without the support of my colleagues at Kennedy Song Dusoir it would have been impossible to find the time for this endeavour, and I owe special thanks to Phil and Jeeun in this regard. Jeeun is also my wife; she has given me more support than anyone. Hauser & Wirth Somerset is a wonderful place populated by helpful, friendly staff and it was a pleasure to spend time there while researching the book. In particular head gardener Mark was incredibly helpful and generous with his knowledge. Thanks also to Piet; it's been a privilege getting to know his work and to have the chance to discuss it with the man himself.

Photo Acknowledgements
The publishers would like to thank the following for use of their photographs:
Toby and Chris Marchant of Orchard Dene Nurseries: 29, 33, 34-5, 40 (left);
Andrew Montgomery 208; Piet Oudolf 181 (bottom right).
All other photographs by Jason Ingram.